Dedicated To Her.

ACKNOWLEDGEMENTS

Mom- Thank you for being my best friend in the Universe. Forever and Always. I love you! xoxoxo

Dad and Rita- Thank you for unconditional love.

To all my pals, you know who you are - Thank you for your loyalty, support and belly laughs.

Russell Simmons- The best self-identified Lesbian straight guy I know. Always great to be the ying to your yang.

Triplicity Publishing (especially Alea Hamilton and Mamie Stevenson)- Thank you for believing.

Stevie, Love, Wanu, Pikachu, Cassidy, Lil Feller, Diablo, Gypsy, Handsome and all the hamsters and mice who live in Heaven- thank you for waiting.

Hubbell Yoda- Thank you for being the best domestic partner a girl could ever ask for.

To my loves- Thank you for the memories and the lessons. Each one of you still holds a sacred place in my heart.

To you, the reader- Thank you for being brave enough to fight or strong enough to let go. May you find the love that completes you and the one who keeps your heart beating faster every day of your life.

And to everyone- Please consider going vegan – for your health, the planet and, of course, the animals.

Slaying the Lesbian Bed Death *Dragon*

(AND being the coolest girlfriend on the planet while you're at it!)

THE 30 Day Guide to Re-Claiming Your Lover

By

Simone Reyes

2015

Slaying the Lesbian Bed Death Dragon © 2015
Simone Reyes
Triplicity Publishing, LLC

ISBN-13: 978-0996899437
ISBN-10: 099689943X

All rights reserved. No part of this book may be reproduced, copied, stored, or transmitted in any form, or by any means—graphic, electronic, or mechanical, including photocopying, or recording—without the prior written permission of Triplicity Publishing, LLC, except where permitted by law.

The information contained in this book is intended to be used as a form of educational, relationship advice. The author and publisher are in no way liable for misuse of the material.

Printed in the United States of America

First Edition – 2015

Cover Design: Triplicity Publishing, LLC

Cover Photo: Lisa Boyle

Cover Image: Patrice Mincey

Interior Design: Triplicity Publishing, LLC

Editor: Mamie Stevenson - Triplicity Publishing, LLC

Table of Contents

Introduction — 1

Part 1: What is Lesbian Bed Death? — 3

Chapter One — 3
Is It Just A Lezzie Thing?

Chapter Two — 15
Is This Book For Me?

Chapter Three — 20
Can Every Relationship Have A " Lessurection"?
Am I Still In Love?
Fall In Love With Yourself
Speak To Your Inner Child
Reacting to Rejection

Part 2: The Thirty-Day Plan to Re-Claim Your Lover (by Being the Coolest Girlfriend on the Planet!) — 38

Chapter Four — 38
Day 1- *Cool Girlfriends Reflect and Keep Journals/Getting in Fighting Shape Mentally*

Chapter Five — 46
Day 2- *Cool Girlfriends Make Connections*

Chapter Six — 50

Day 3- *Cool Girlfriends Look Hot from Head to Toe*
Chapter Seven 67
Day 4- *Cool Girlfriend Look Ultra Sexy " Down There"*
Chapter Eight 71
Day 5- *Cool Girlfriends Give Compliments- and Clues of What's To Come*
Chapter Nine 75
Day 6- *Cool Girlfriends Leave Hidden Notes*
Chapter Ten 77
Day 7- *Cool Girlfriends Flirt (But Save The Last Dance for their Woman)*
Chapter Eleven 85
Day 8- Cool *Girlfriends Spoil Their Woman Good*
Chapter Twelve 90
Day 9- *Cool Girlfriends Know How to Prep A Room for Seduction*
Chapter Thirteen 95
Day 10- *Cool Girlfriends Dig The Spook*
Chapter Fourteen 98
Day 11- Cool *Girlfriend's Kiss Their Woman as if She is Going Off to Wa*r
Chapter Fifteen 101
Day 12- *Cool Girlfriends Send Flowers*
Chapter Sixteen 105
Day 13- *Cool Girlfriends Go Commando*

Chapter Seventeen   **109**
Day 14- *Cool Girlfriends Take Their Girlfriend on Cool Adventures*

Chapter Eighteen   **112**
Day 15- *Cool Girlfriends Know How to Serve Dinner Right*

Chapter Nineteen   **116**
Day 16- *Cool Girlfriends Speak Erotically – Tell her Somethin' Good*

Chapter Twenty   **122**
Day 17- *Cool Girlfriends Watch Porn*

Chapter Twenty-One   **125**
Day 18- *Cool Girlfriends Like to Watch and Be Watched*

Chapter Twenty-Two   **129**
Day 19- *Cool Girlfriends Have Got Pole- Will Strip (and Give Lap Dances!)*

Chapter Twenty-Three   **151**
Day 20- *Let The Games Begin*

Chapter Twenty- Four   **153**
Day 21- *Cool Girlfriends Give Gifts To Feed The Spirit*

Chapter Twenty- Five   **155**
Day 22- *Cool Girlfriends Give Back*

Chapter Twenty-Six   **158**
Day 23- *Cool Girlfriend's Conserve Water and Shower Together*

Chapter Twenty-Seven   **160**
Day 24- *Cool Girlfriends Book Hotel Sex*
Chapter Twenty-Eight   **163**
Day 25- *Cool Girlfriends Make Videos*
Chapter Twenty-Nine   **166**
Day 26- *Cool Girlfriends Plan Yearly Honeymoons*
Chapter Thirty   **168**
Day 27- *Cool Girlfriends Eat Out*
Chapter Thirty-One   **171**
Day 28- *Cool Girlfriends Go Shopping – Strap-Ons, Butt Plugs, and Edible Panties OH MY!*
Chapter Thirty- Two   **178**
Day 29- *Cool Girlfriends Dig Quickies*
Chapter Thirty-Three   **180**
Day 30- *Cool Girlfriends Play Twister Every Night*
Chapter Thirty-Four   **188**
Day 31- *Cool Girlfriends Have Great Sex*

Part 3: I've Got My Lover Back….Now What?   **191**
Cool Girlfriends Keep The Fire Burning
What If Issues Still Remain?

About the Author   **200**

Simone Reyes

Introduction

One night I had a dream…

It was early evening on a warm, balmy day on an island paradise. Two women were sitting on the sand at dusk. One woman was wearing a sheer, toga styled lavender dress. She had matching ribbons tied into her long flowing, brown hair. She was beautiful. The other woman was Wonder Woman (in full superhero attire wearing a red bustier, gold plated eagle breast plate, gold headband, bullet deflecting bracelets, magic lasso, red and white striped boots- the whole ensemble). In my dream state I realized it must be THE Paradise Island where Amazon women excelled at sports, worshipped Goddesses and lived harmoniously together. It certainly looked like paradise to me. They had set the perfect romantic scene with a crackling fire, romantic music and a basket of strawberries. The women were engaged in a lively conversation and occasionally held hands. They looked very comfortable with each other and it was clear by their body language they were a couple. As the night grew darker—and the moon brighter—the two women finished the last of the fruit. They both smiled at each other and laid themselves down on a blanket on the

Slaying the Lesbian Bed Death Dragon

warm sand under the night sky. With a peck on the cheek they turned to face opposite sides of the island and drifted off to sleep.

This is where the dream turned into a nightmare. A nightmare that is all too familiar in long term lesbian relationships. Even Wonder Woman it seemed, with all her magical super powers, was not strong enough to slay the Lesbian Bed Death Dragon.

That's where this book comes in. I may not be a card-carrying superhero (although I have been known to dress up like one on occasion just for fun), but I have created a thirty-day plan that I firmly believe will reignite the flame in your relationship and send that dragon packing.

All I ask of you is to keep an open mind and follow the plan as closely as you can. At the end of this book, you will be strapping yourself into your invisible plane and heading home to Paradise Island into the open, loving arms of your girlfriend/wife. And the sex, oh the sex…. honey, will be HOT!

Simone Reyes

PART I: What is Lesbian Bed Death?

Chapter One

Is It Just A Lezzie Thing?

The dreaded Lesbian Bed Death Syndrome. Ugh, just the mere mention of it sends a shiver down my spine —and probably yours too! As most lesbians know, "bed death" is a term that became popular when invented by sex researcher Pepper Schwartz. She invented the term to describe the supposedly inevitable diminution of sexual passion in long term lesbian relationships. Schwartz's published findings indicate lesbian couples have less sexual contact than those of any other sexual orientation, even co-habitating / married heterosexual couples and gay male couples.

This is a hotly debated topic in the lesbian community with many calling the term unfair and fraudulent. Frankly, it doesn't matter all that much to me if lesbians are the leader in the "not tonight, honey" parade or not. Why? Because if Lesbian Bed Death (or for those that don't want to validate the term—lack of sexual appetite) has found your address and bunked down in your bedroom, that monster is not leaving any time soon unless we blow it out of the water. LBD causes pain, stress and distance between partners and it needs to be attacked head on if the relationship is going to survive for the long haul. You and your girlfriend/wife will need powerful tools to accomplish this. It's not a journey for cowards. But it CAN be done. And this superhero is dashing to the rescue to offer her help. Period.

In fairness to the debate, I will say that I personally believe that in ALL relationships, hetero/gay/etc., it can be a tall order to keep the passion alive after the newness of a relationship wears off. In off and on relationships that thrive on the chase, once the prize is caught it's not uncommon to fall into a rut. Typically at this stage relationships end or partners decide to "fix" it by getting hitched. Of course, as many of us have experienced, leaving a relationship based on sex alone isn't ideal but neither is getting married a way to fix what is broken. Lesbians, like all other couples, meet, fall in love (and delicious lust), rent a U-haul, move in and spend a lovely, magical amount of time getting to know everything about their new love. We spend every waking moment on the phone, sending text messages and emails, creating music playlists for each other, exchanging gifts and getting to know what makes our new girlfriend tick. We inquire about her ex girlfriends/sometimes ex-boyfriends, her parents, her childhood, her coming out, her triumphs, losses and dreams. We spend countless nights exploring every inch of her exquisite body, making love until dawn and then repeating this over and over again. We look at her photos on Instagram and screen shot them, sending them to our friends to brag about. We post endless photos of her on social media after having decided she is by far the best looking girl we have ever seen and show her off to the world. We learn what our lover desires, what she fears, what her fantasies are, what her hang ups are—the whole shebang. Then, slowly over time, real life creeps in. We suddenly realize that the dishes are piling up in the kitchen; there are one hundred email messages that need to be returned; we have used up all our sick days; we are ignoring our friends and our careers because we just can't seem to stop making love to this beautiful creature.

So, eventually (and against our will) we pull our naked, tired bodies out of bed and begin to deal with the stress of paying our rent/mortgage, excelling at our jobs, running our businesses, dealing with various health issues, taking care of elderly parents, giving love to demanding companion animals, having babies, getting laid off, getting rehired, redecorating, doing the laundry, maintaining friendships, etc. All of these sometimes mundane—but always important—life chores demand our full attention. Unfortunately, tending to these details often leave casualties in their wake. Most often, the casualty is the sexual intimacy we share with our partner. We get tired, stressed, busy—but not in the fun way of "getting busy". Weeks turn into months and eventually years where two women suddenly find themselves laying in bed together facing opposite walls wondering, "When was the last time we made love?" The answer is often scary, shocking and painful. And what's worse, it is quite frequently never discussed— let alone worked on.

Some people may disagree with me, but I do believe that women are infinitely different from men and therefore, what happens in our relationships are vastly different as well. I have found that women can feel intimately connected to their partner even when LBD is "in the house", so to speak. We often draw on our deep friendship, intimacy, familiarity, as well as our emotional, intellectual and spiritual connections to bond us to our partner. When we are holding hands with our girlfriend, feeling her spooning us in bed and having a good time with her overall, we often dismiss the dwindling down or complete lack of sex as "normal". We begin to rely on other means of coping— showering our kids with all of our attention, drinking more, building our empires, etc. Men, in my opinion, are much more likely to read this as a clear signal that there is a problem and often try to initiate sex with their partner. They may even be more likely to self-medicate with an affair. We are simply different than men and therefore need to use different tools to get us back in the sack.

For example, studies have shown that adult men under 60 think about sex at least once a day. Only about one quarter of women say they think of sex that frequently. Roy Baumeister, a social psychologist at Florida State University, shared the results of studies in a review that found many ways women's sexual attitudes, practices and desires were more influenced by their environment as compared to men. This includes, but isn't limited to, women being more influenced by the opinions of their peer group about sex and their religious habits (women who attend church more regularly, for example, are more likely than men to be permissive about sex). Biologically speaking, men's sex drives are seemingly more tied to their biology than women's. Braunstein says, " There is a hormonal factor in (sex drive) but it's much more evident in men than women."

Women, on the other hand, can be terrific communicators and support systems for each other. However, in a situation where LBD is an issue it can also be self-sabotaging. As women, we often find we are acutely sensitive to feelings and therefore many of us find it uncomfortable to initiate sex if we feel that our partner isn't feeling it. Many women will probably agree that nothing cuts quite as deep as sexual rejection. As partners, we understand and sympathize with her and don't want to put any additional pressure on her or the relationship. There is also something to be said for the fact that no matter how awesome our strap on maybe it's not a real penis and it doesn't have a mind of its own (as some could argue the male penis may have.) Our sexual organs are on the inside and sometimes it may seem harder to reach literally and figuratively. It doesn't exactly salute us first thing in the morning to give us an indication of what may be going on down below.

For a woman, sexual thoughts typically start in the mind. If our desire is to truly engage our woman then we need to first arouse her mind—her body will follow.

A study by Louann Brizendine of the University of California in San Francisco found that for men foreplay is everything that occurs in the three minutes prior to insertion. For women, she found it's everything that happens in the 24 hours beforehand. That is where this book comes in. Sure, I could have you jump to ahead to a chapter towards the end of the 30 day plan, instruct you to put on something risqué and tell you to give your girl a lap dance or woo her with flowers and a few shots of Tequila on your anniversary while whispering sweet nothings in her ear, which most likely will get your woman aroused, but I don't want you to just heat up her flame. I want you to set her flame ablaze so that it will stay lit forever and that will require you to crawl inside her brain. Getting inside is no easy feat; our minds are often clogged up with so many thoughts that sex can easily fall to the bottom of that pile.

Add this to the mix- as women we also tend to over-analyze everything and simply love to talk issues to death— to Lesbian Bed Death! Then, there is PMS: women get hormonal and emotional each month during which time we are bloated, irritable and have cramps. Often we sync up with our girlfriends and are both "on the rag" at the same time. When you do the math, it's no surprise that LBD (or a lull in desire) is running so rampant in our community—we have a lot to contend with as women! We also often feel we have to work twice as hard as men, typically for less pay, to get ahead. We are expected to raise our children and have a career without complaining. Being a woman is hard work and we are still fighting for equality in many areas of our lives.

Instead of looking LBD in the eye and making an effort to identify and overcome it, many women often just shrug it away and sweep it under the rug along with our daily housekeeping. That dirt has a way of collecting over time and it eventually becomes a big old dust monster under our bed. Granted, after a few years in a monogamous relationship, a decrease or lack of sexual intimacy may seem common. However, I don't think we should automatically label it as acceptable, especially when sex becomes a treat instead of a familiar and expected gift. When a woman (or two women) decides that loss of sexual desire is par for the course, I truly believe they are in denial. We inherently know, deep down, that we are all sexual beings and that it is healthy to desire our partner sexually. We know in our gut that something is missing from our lives if we aren't getting it on a regular basis.

However, LBD so often goes long ignored, that once it is finally addressed, the problem seems so monumental that curing it seems hopeless. I once visited a psychic during a particularity long stretch of sadness. She looked at me and said that my sadness was a part of my life for so long that there would be no easy way to snap out of it. She said that my body had "forgotten" how to make serotonin. She likened it to someone having an arm injury and wearing a cast for a year. Then, someone breaks off the cast and asks this person to suddenly throw a winning curve ball. Their muscles have begun to atrophy and the arm is in many ways useless. However, with proper care and slow muscle building exercises it can work again. It's the same with sexual passion- we just need to give some special care to the problem and one day soon it will be good as new. This is how I view the loss of sexual desire by one or both partners. Easing back into ecstasy will yield much higher returns than forcing a crash into it. Trust me!.

The first way to begin to exercise that arm is to address that there is a problem with it. I have found that LBD is rarely discussed because it carries a stigma of shame. We often feel embarrassed that we have infrequent sex (or aren't making love at all anymore) with our woman. We don't want to appear like our relationship is in trouble so we hide it. Lesbian communities are often so small that gossip such as this tends to spread like a wildfire. Lesbians also tend to date within their small circle of friends so regardless of how evolved we are, it's simply not comfortable to announce to our girlfriend's ex that we aren't "doing it" on a regular basis. However, hidden or not, it is my firm belief that LBD simply must be addressed and conquered. If it is not, its presence leaves the door open to feelings of inadequacy, shame, self-loathing and of course can lead to infidelity. This is not to say, however, that any of the aforementioned issues will definitely happen, but in my opinion, LBD leaves a path clear for them to invade the relationship. Once something like infidelity has occurred, it is often too late to repair the lack of trust. There is a saying that trust is like a piece of paper, once it's crumpled its never the same again.

On the topic of infidelity, we can easily become confused when a stranger suddenly elicits a sexual response from us. A woman who is self-confidant can make the woman they are hitting on feel beautiful again—a feeling that many LBD syndrome sufferers don't readily identify with. It can be very flattering to feel wanted and desired by another female. When we don't feel lusted after by our mate, trouble is on the horizon. How easy it is to incorrectly assume that this new person is "The One" and that our girlfriend was the once upon a time. This is a sad and unnecessary outcome to a problem that can often be solved by engaging in some honest communication and by doing the exercises in this book. Attention from another person doesn't necessarily mean that they value you, nor does it mean they are worth leaving a committed relationship for.

There are also people in the world who are masters at manipulation and prey on couples who are struggling. I don't mean to generalize or put fear into you, but I do want you to recognize that if you don't proactively try to protect your relationship there are some unsavory individuals who may try to swoop in, confuse the situation and walk away with one half of the couple now on their arm. Those stories don't just happen in soap operas. Chances are in your friend pool someone has made a move on a partner in a committed relationship and tested the waters. Everyone can be vulnerable to feeling excited by new attention if we aren't feeling wanted at home. However, trust is of paramount importance in a relationship. Once the trust has been broken it can be nearly impossible to put Humpty Dumpty back together again. This isn't just in the case of infidelity but emotional cheating can leave deep scars as well. Love isn't a prize to be won. Don't gamble it away—you could lose someone very precious to you to another who is unworthy of either of you. Always keep an eye open for these individuals; chances are they have used their manipulation in the past to break up other relationships. That is always a huge red flag.

In conclusion, is LBD a lezzie thing? Who cares? If it's your thing and it's causing you pain and threatening your relationship, it needs to be cured. And it WILL BE. Or you will realize the problem isn't just sex. Either way, there will be healing. I promise.

*As a brief but important side note, I must briefly address safe sex. Lesbian Bed Death Syndrome primarily happens in long-term monogamous lesbian relationships. Therefore, I am going to assume that because both of you have entered into such a relationship that you have discussed your sexual histories and have been tested for HIV and STDs. Of course, if you haven't taken care of these vital tests and exchanged this pertinent information, I urge you to do so immediately. Until then, please use caution and introduce latex gloves, condoms (for dildos) and dental dams into your world. Sex is sexy. Safe sex is sexier (and just may save your life).

Chapter Two

Is This Book For Me?

Cool girlfriends don't get hooked on labels. Whether you consider yourself old-school/classic butch, femme, power femme, femme top, femme bottom, butch top, butch bottom, baby butch, baby femme, androgynies, stud and lady, packing butch, high femme, daddy/girl, mommy/boy, stone femme, stone butch, polyamorous, fag butch, andro dyke, gender-bender, genderfuck, transgendered, etc. I feel completely confident that you will be able to follow the plan while maintaining your sense of self.

That said, I don't want to pretend that the no-touch butch doesn't exist. In many strictly S/M couples, I know how important it is to stick to the old rules that have been around for a very long time. I don't want any of my readers to feel that they have to change who they are to get their girlfriend interested in sex again. However, being open to pushing your boundaries and traveling out of your comfort zone can only be beneficial to you both. I firmly believe that every lesbian—while still allowing room for your own personal touches—can carry out every assignment in this book successfully. I have provided many alternatives to each part of the plan to ensure every woman can play while feeling like herself.

While I will make quite a few suggestions on important changes you will need to consider making—not only in your personal appearance but in your everyday life, I will never ask you to change who you are. Your girlfriend fell in love with you for who you are. Now you just need to polish up that person and rediscover that person as she is now. Chances are you have lost a little bit of her along the way. I will help you find her; she is there hibernating inside your soul… we just have to re-awaken her.

You must always remember that the essence of who you are is perfect and I will keep reminding you of this lest you forget. Some of us may enjoy taking on a more traditional "male" role of being the main driver, carrying the heavier groceries, making most of the plans and being the one who is mainly the top gal. Some of us simply feel more comfortable when we embrace our masculine side and feel the most like ourselves, and at our most sexy, with no makeup on, short haircuts and converse sneakers (and sometimes even packin' a sexy surprise under our jeans). Baby, that is hot.

On the other side of the coin, some of us prefer to embrace the more classically feminine, maternal part of the couple. Some of us love to have our hair blown out once a week, wear long flowing nightgowns to bed and high heels to work every day. We prefer to be the bottom chick most of the time. Baby, that is hot too.

Some of us enjoy dating someone who looks like our polar opposite; some of us date our twin. Some go for a girl that looks like a typical tall, blond-haired trophy wife or while others prefer the no makeup, girl-next-door types. Some of us switch it up and just go with the flow. There are no rules. We come in all shapes, types and sizes—thank goodness! While at first glance this book may seem to be geared more toward the lipstick/femme, the counterpart is always going to be addressed in every chapter. I have seen the most butch girl tap into her femme side to make the woman she loves feel like she's in the driver's seat. We have all heard the "butch in the streets, femme in the sheets" cliché, well, sometimes that is exactly how it is. I have also seen the most femme/lipstick lesbians pull out their power moves and push their woman up against a wall and have their way with her, being the aggressor. We are all a magical mix of masculine and feminine energy. Therefore, let's throw the labels out the window and accept that we are all beautifully complex creatures who can surprise our woman -and ourselves- from time to time.

My point is that nobody is just one persona. Sure we all have our tendencies, and we are all familiar with the essence of who we are, but women are chameleons with many changing sides. Some nights you may really want to be the bottom chick, but the next morning you may be the top—or better yet, practice playing both all night long. Hey, whatever floats your boat! I have written this book to help every lesbian embrace the person they are and help them reclaim their lover. And why do I feel that I am the best choice to write this book? Well, first because I know what it's like to lie awake at night watching my partner sleep, wondering if the last time we kissed was the last time. Instead of just staring at the wall, I decided to do something about it.

I also know what it's like to treat my partner like royalty— lavishing gifts, attention and showering them with the biggest most all consuming love this side of the

Mississippi. When the ebbs were longer than the free flowing times of sexual desire, I had to really try to find my own strength to be brave enough to reach out for something I feared was lost forever. I had to go into my bag of tricks and create magic again in my relationship. I had to be brave. I had to be willing to fail while expecting to dazzle. I had to show my love that they chose the right girl, and that I was indeed the best girlfriend on the planet, even if we lost our way in the bedroom. And I succeeded because I did the work. I allowed myself to be vulnerable and get my lover to desire me again and again. I went the extra mile because I knew that our shared intimacy and unbroken trust in each other was strong despite a lull in our libidos. I knew the relationship had a foundation sturdy enough to support us through a difficult journey. In other relationships, I also knew when to walk away. But most importantly, I knew that no matter what the end result, I would never have any regrets because I always acted out of pure love and gave my relationship 100%. I completely dedicated myself to those that let me into their heart and allowed me in to rock their world.

Chapter Three

Can Every Relationship Have a "Lessurection"?

Many of you may be wondering if your sex life can ever be resurrected or "lessurected"? If there is love present, then the resounding answer is YES! I know how easy it is to believe that our relationship may have progressed so far into a sexless partnership that it simply is too late to revive. Quiet those fears, the healing is well on the way!

You may also be asking yourself why this book isn't addressed as a couples therapy guide, with both partners reading along together and carrying out exercises as a pair. You may be saying under your breath, "Why do I have to do all the work?" Sorry, but (a) hey, someone has to be the bareback (b) one person always wants to initiate change just a tad more than the other and (c) I promise you that once you see the positive changes in your woman it will spill right over to your libido and you will get just as turned on as your woman—probably even more so! One fire ignites the other like a brush fire. It's just science, ladies.

In all seriousness, it can seem scary to embark on this journey. It may feel as if you are putting yourself in vulnerable situations and setting yourself up for rejection- all without a net. To a point, you are correct, but remember it is sexy to be brave. The only regrets I have in life are the chances I didn't take, the words I never spoke and the love I never shared. There have been grave miscommunications that have contributed to the end of some of my relationships that I know could have been avoided had I been brave enough to speak my truth. My pride often got in the way of real communication (it's the Leo in me). However, I recognize this and have worked on it. Nobody is perfect—I certainly am not. Making ourselves open to injury is part of healing but keep in mind, this is not a stranger you are opening yourself up to. The woman you are bowing down before—with your heart on a platter—is YOUR woman. Your girlfriend/wife loves you, even if she isn't touching you in a sexual way every day. I bet she touches your heart every day. Your mate is beside you in this life, so trust her. Trust yourself.

Slaying the Lesbian Bed Death Dragon

I won't spend a lot of time covering reasons, other than the ones outlined earlier, as to why LBD (or whatever term you feel comfortable using) may have found your house. However, these issues must be considered. We must ask ourselves to look deeply into our subconscious and ask ourselves if negative experiences from our past (or present) are manifesting themselves into carriers of LBD. These issues include (but are not limited to) child abuse, sexual abuse, menopause, homophobia and homosexual shame or embarrassment, cultural stereotypes of beauty, self-image issues, etc. If you suspect that one of these issues is at the core of your (or your partner's) LBD issue, I urge you to seek therapy. It will be very helpful to first come to terms with those big demons that are cluttering up your closets and contributing to your inability to have frequent physical relations with your partner. After you have identified the demon, understand its origin and the way it is affecting your sex life you can decide how to proceed with therapy or support groups, etc. Then, pick up this book and carry out the thirty- day plan.

This book is not a quick fix. We are all complicated, ever-evolving women. It is natural for everyone to carry around baggage from our childhood or past relationships that continue to cause issues in our lives. It is not, however, healthy to ignore that baggage. Issues will always swing around and bite us in the asso, please go within and begin your healing. Call in professional help if needed. There is never shame in asking for assistance. Join a support group. Speak to a counselor. Remember that your lover is there to support you and in no time at all, she will also be there in a physical way to make you feel safe, loved, cherished and turned on.

Am I Still In Love?

Only you can answer this question. When couples aren't connecting in a sexual way this question certainly arises. Many of you are asking yourselves "Can I go on living this way?" "Am I happy in the relationship overall?" "Does she still love me?" "What is wrong with me?" "Has my lover turned into my sister?" "Am I asexual?" " Have we fallen out of love?"

Pretty scary stuff, huh. When doing research for this book I found in one survey that 15% of married couples haven't had (or have had very little) sexual contact with their mate during the past year. Sexless is a term usually measured by less than ten sexual connections a year. The numbers are typically higher in lesbian relationships. There are many varying opinions as to why this happens. Aging is not as large a factor as some may assume. Many of those who are going through bed death in their relationships are considered young by any standards—couples in their twenties experience sexless relationships as well.

In a study found in *Why Women Have Sex* (Times Books), by sex researchers David M. Buss, PhD, and Cindy M. Meston, PhD, 32 percent of women aged 18 - 24 (single and married) reported having little interest in sex in the past year. This was taken from a sample of over 1,700 women. This illustrates that there are many issues at play when it comes to sexual activity, not just the often go-to assumption that the union is doomed or dead.

Monogamy can put a lot of pressure on some lesbians who had many years of either a lot of sex or different kinds of sex with multiple partners. Is it possible that you came into the relationship expecting nightly fireworks and got disappointed? Sure. Is there a chance that part of your sexual turn-ons involve seeing a different vagina every few weeks? Possibly. Are you addicted to the hormonal high of those first few months or the first year when your heart is beating out of your chest every time your girl says your name? Who isn't? Those feelings rule. However, can they be a constant in our lives forever? Probably not in the same way, but we can certainly work on it. Everyone deserves fireworks.

The idea of being in love is also confusing. Are we in love with the person this woman was when we moved in together and not who she is now? Are we in love with keeping our family together if we have children or companion animals verses what the family dynamic is in reality? Are we in love with being supported financially if we married a woman who has more money? Are we in love with our shared history and friendship? Are we in love with "winning her" from other women, even if it was all about the game versus the person? All of these questions have true answers and you must be strong enough to address them honestly. Loving someone and being in love are totally different actions. Ask yourself if you can imagine your life without this person as your bride? Is she the end all to you? Is there someone from your past who could still steal you away? Would you take a bullet for her? Are you proud to show her off? Is she your equal? Is she the one that you envision your kids being just like? Does she walk in a room and make you weak in the knees? Does she challenge you? Teach you? Inspire you? Do you value her advice over all others? Do you trust her with your life? Has she treated you as you deserve to be treated? Are you confident she won't ever cheat on you? Do you like yourself when you are with her? Does she compliment you? Do you walk in a room with her on your arm and feel like the most lucky girl in the place? Do you believe she would never deceive you? Do you count on being with her forever?

These questions may help you decide if you are still in love or were ever in love with your woman. I feel confident that if you are brave and honest with yourself you will find your answer. I can tell you this: if you don't love yourself you can't truly love your woman. If you haven't made peace with being alone and not always coupled up, you cannot expect to know if it's real love or not. You absolutely must be comfortable with yourself first. Since you are in a relationship, it may seem to be a bit late in the game to begin exploring loving your own company without the crutch of a live-in lover, but it's never too late to love yourself.

Fall In Love With Yourself:

I want you in fighting shape for this battle so let's focus for a moment on the concept of loving yourself.

Self-love is one of the most important tools in your arsenal of slaying the Bed Death Dragon. You must be willing to accept yourself while committing to the belief that you are a work in progress and be willing to make changes to better yourself. In the end, all we have is our own reflection, whether we are standing next to our lover or not. That reflection must be someone we are proud to know.

In order to get you to this place please allow me to offer you some suggestions on loving yourself.

Re-connect with your friends. Often when we couple up we get so wrapped up in this new person or so comfortable in our domestic life we lose track of the friends that were there for us before we became part of a couple. Sometimes we become BFFs with all of her circle of friends and neglect our own. We must be conscious to keep our relationships strong. Not only are friends good sounding boards, but they are great stress relievers and anti-depressants. Go have FUN with your friends and don't feel obligated to always bring your girlfriend or wife along. We each need to maintain and cultivate friendships outside of our relationship. Of course you want to remain respectful of your significant other but don't feel guilty having some alone time with your girls. Assure your girl there is no need for her to feel jealous or threatened. Remind her that you come home to her every night. Also encourage your girl to reconnect with her friends. Group outings can be a great way of socializing but we all need our time away as well.

-On the flip side, spend time by yourself. Take yourself out to a movie, a spa day, learn to meditate and set time aside to binge watch a series your mate probably wouldn't enjoy. Read books, join meet-up groups of like minded people and take your dogs out for walks where it is time for just you and your furry companion(s). Learn to love it.

-Ease up on yourself. Give yourself a break. Ok, so that presentation didn't win you the account. So, you said the wrong thing to your mother-in-law about her homemade pie and now she gives you the stink eye even after you apologized. Your alarm made you miss your morning workout? Things happen. Not everything is your fault. Move on.

-Practice forgiveness. Yes, your ex strung you along for years and never settled down with you. Yes, your first sexual encounter was with someone who never spoke to you again. Yes, your parents were absent in your formative years and sometimes forget to call you on your birthday. Yes your assistant ran off with your accountant leaving you high and dry. Yes your girlfriend just charged a new outfit on your joint credit card without discussing it and put you over the limit. Whatever it is, view if from a place of forgiveness. This is not to say that you can't express your dissatisfaction with any of these people but don't hold on to the anger. Anger has a way of festering and destroying our own inner peace. Some will argue it makes us a target for disease. It certainly will affect your happiness. Let go and move on.

-Get a hobby. Start collecting something that you love—trading cards from your childhood? Original movie posters? Take an acting class! Write that novel! Certainly there is something you have never done but would love to do!

-Dance like nobody is watching. Turn on the music when you are alone and go crazy. Celebrate all that is going well for you right now; let go of what isn't and dance it out!

-Make it a priority to smile. When we are sad, we can go a very long time without smiling. Start to practice the art of smiling. I guarantee your mood will lift. Smile at nature, at strangers and at every living being around you. This will come back in waves. Smiling is contagious.

-Don't be judgmental. Everyone is imperfect. We are all struggling in our own way. You will be happier if you try to right the wrongs of the world without throwing rocks at everyone you disagree with.

-Seek out and make peace with people from your past. You will find that once you have reached out to anyone who you still have unresolved issues with and clear the air with them, you will be a happier person.

-Stop being a people pleaser. Learn to say NO when you feel overextended. Remember it's better to do something out of love than to do it filled with resentment. Saying no sometimes is saying yes to yourself. You can't be everywhere or fix everything. Do the best you can.

Speak to your Inner Child

Simone Reyes

This exercise will help exorcise some self-sabotaging demons that may be lying in wait to make the next month a lot more difficult.

First imagine yourself as a small child. What is she doing? Smiling? Crying? Examine her home life. Is it supported? Peaceful? Loud? How is she feeling? Is she content? Lonely? Scared? Angry? Does she have a mother and a father in her life? Is she from a broken home? Does she get along with her siblings? Does she wish she had a brother or a sister to play with? Does she have a companion animal? Does she feel safe? Are her needs being taken care of? Is her household healthy or destructive? Is she happy or sad? What is her belief system? Does she believe she is worthy of love? Does she believe everything is her fault? What lessons about life did she learn from her parent's relationship? Did she suffer from personal abuse? Were there external circumstances like divorce imprinted onto her?

Taking the time to recognize what felt normal to you as a child can be a vital tool in helping you to stop repeating patterns that are unhealthy for you or your partner. During formative years we imprint a lot more than we may realize. Trauma doesn't just go away, it lives inside of us and often comes out in the way we treat our lovers and ourselves. Traumatized children may fixate on past hurts and grow up destined to repeat these feelings making sure to re-create them by any means necessary. Many traumatized people (whether the trauma was of the painful personal variety such as physical/emotional abuse or the hurt of surviving a death in the family / parental divorce, etc.) expose themselves, seemingly compulsively, to situations reminiscent of the original trauma. Some women can scan a room of attractive, eligible women who are all relatively healthy prospects for a relationship and unconsciously zero in on the one who is most likely to break her heart. I used to be that woman. I usually joked that I was a like a bull, in that red flags attracted me. I did a lot of work on myself and no longer do I search for the one emotionally unavailable person in the room.

I am a work in progress but after years of co-dependent and unhealthy relationships, I have come to realize that they will never make me feel whole or satisfied. Relationships such as these keep us repeating old habits and patterns that invite in pain and discontent to our lives. After years of this not so merry-go-round relationships, I finally realized that I am able to make loving decisions on who I should be with or not be with that will ultimately provide the highest good for both of us. I am no longer in the headspace to beat myself up and neither should you be.

Honest, raw self-reflection is difficult but the good news is we know ourselves better than anyone. Consider for a moment the advice you would give yourself if you were your own best friend. Think of all the things you would remind yourself of and the examples from your past you would use to drive your point home. If we don't take responsibility for our own happiness and past mistakes, we will continue to choose mates that we believe are the love of our lives who still make us feel nervous, angry, afraid, distrustful or just plain bad. And yet we stay in the relationship knowing in our gut this isn't what love is supposed to feel like. Or sometimes we do convince ourselves this is love because it's all we know of love. What we can't consciously feel can still have tremendous power over us. If our childhood contained high levels of emotional pain, stress and anger we may find ourselves moving into adult roles carrying unconscious or only partially conscious baggage that we aren't fully aware of. This baggage will ultimately interfere with how we relate to our partners. Unresolved pain from the past, especially our formative years, gets transferred onto the relationships that shape our destiny. And the sad result is that our genuine reactions to previous painful events may be unavailable to us, hidden even from our own sane /conscious thought. Often we are unable to trace our inappropriate reactions to the situations in our lives presently, to their origins from our childhood. I can especially relate to not understanding in the heat of the moment that our intense emotional reactions to what is happening in the present belong entirely to the memory that is triggering them.

So often we are unconscious of what might be driving us to act out from that place of pain that is in our past. Over-reacting in the present is often triggered by a trauma in our past that has little to do with what is today's trigger but we seldom recognize that. We lash out at our partner, have a panic attack, feel anxious or furious momentarily because our pain from the past is being triggered leaving us feeling out of control and our partner confused and blindsided by our reactions. Usually, and in our defense, pivotal fragments of the original traumatic event have become inaccessible to memory. This is where we need to stop and reflect. When our partner does something that hurts us, makes us feel taken for granted or disrespected, we may fly into a rage surprising even ourselves. This kind of behavior can put a lot of stress on a partnership and while it may be the voice of a scared, angry, hysterical child calling out for help in our own psyche, it appears as misdirected anger towards our partner. Recognizing the voice of that child is the first step. Going to therapy or employing other healing modalities to aid that inner child is critical. Your lover can't always be expected to dismiss these kinds of blow-ups. She shouldn't have to. Do the work on yourself that will help free you from this destructive behavior. If it is your partner who is acting out in similar ways, calmly call her out on it and tell her that you support her but that she needs to consider doing what she can to help heal that inner child.

Love and care gently for the child that is still suffering in so many of us. Get her the help she needs. When she starts to come through, you can imagine yourself as that wounded child as you whisper in her ear and gently rock her in your arms. Tell her she is loved unconditionally and that you are so proud of her. Let her know that she is all grown up now and that you hear her calling to you and understand her rage and pain but those emotions aren't healthy for you anymore. Surround her with white light and love. Then release her.

Reacting To Rejection

Rejection is part of life. It doesn't mean you are less than, unattractive, stupid, un-cool or unworthy. You are embarking on a journey that is bound to deliver you some humbling moments. You will be wearing your heart on your sleeve and making plans to get closer to your lover even if you don't feel hot for her. Nobody said this would be easy! If you are doing an exercise and your girlfriend /wife looks at you like you are crazy, it is bound to knock you off balance. Accept that rejection is not just a possibility but also a probability. If the roles were reversed you may find yourself just as likely to shun her sexual moves because you both are in the grips of the dragon. However, you made the move first to try to remedy the situation. Pride has its place. If you are a Leo like me, it holds too big a place in your life. You should never allow anyone to strip you of your pride to the point of belittling you or humiliating you. However, taking a chance and getting knocked down a few times are a part of life. If something matters enough we show up prepared to get hit a few times. Survivors fall down but they don't quit. Fight for your love. She may reject your advances a few times. If so, try to have faith in the end result. If every time you try to get closer you are met with a slammed door then the problem may be bigger than just a lack of sexual passion. That is something that you will need to examine after the month is up. For now, believe this plan will work and it will.

PART 2: The Thirty-Day Plan to Re-claim Your Lover
(By Being the Coolest Girlfriend on the Planet!)

Chapter Four

Day 1- Cool Girlfriends Reflect and Keep Journals/Getting in Fighting Shape Mentally

How exciting! Welcome to the first day of lesbian relationship boot camp! This is the day where I ask you to go out and buy a journal. Be sure to make it a large thick one. The journal is going to be your other girlfriend, your sounding board, your secret keeper, your best friend, your everything for at least thirty days, and hopefully for life. Many things are going to be changing for you. You are going to be embarking on an exciting, new adventure to re-capture something that has been lost. Sometimes it will be exhilarating, sometimes frightening and sometimes you will feel helpless and angry. All of these emotions are expected. However, expressing all our feelings, as they occur, is often a recipe for a relationship disaster. How many times have you felt hurt by your girl and it comes out as anger? Often when our mate does something that wounds us, we lash out in pain disguised as anger. We yell at her or cry. We feel attacked and make her feel guilty. Looking back at our indulgence, we feel sad, regretful and sorry. We usually wish we had counted to twenty before we reacted to whatever was upsetting us. Think of this journal as your "count to twenty" free-pass. When you are feeling rejected, which certainly may happen during the next month in particular, don't get angry—go to your journal and write down what is going on in your head. Try very hard to bite your tongue and go straight to your journal before you express yourself all over your woman. Write down exactly what you are feeling, how you feel about your girlfriend, what you want to happen, etc. I guarantee you will both be better off for it.

This month is going to be filled with emotions that fall all over the map. Feelings are sure to come up that you aren't prepared to face alone and that is where the journal comes in. You may find yourself writing about your insecurities, fears, joy, pride—the list is endless. In time, you may also find that during tough and troubling times you will go to your journal first before you say or do anything you may regret. This will be the most important gift the journal will give you. Outbursts, crying spells and the blame game are part of relationships, but they never do anyone any good.

Please don't misunderstand me: I don't want you to feel that you can't be honest and express yourself to your girlfriend. She does need to know how you are feeling and I would never suggest you hide from her. However, I urge you to write down your feelings in your journal whenever you are experiencing an emotion that you know is going to cause stress to the relationship. We don't want your anxiety or insecurity to throw you three steps back when you are making strides in the right direction.

Use your journal as a sounding board first and I promise you that when you share your feelings with your girl, you will do so in a calmer, saner way. It may feel strange to be sharing an uncomfortable moment with your woman, feeling that familiar rise of emotions in your throat. You will find yourself getting ready to open your mouth, not knowing what will fly out and then rushing off to throw it all down in a journal before anything is verbalized. Yes, it will feel odd but eventually it will come as naturally as brushing your teeth.

Simone Reyes

We must treat our women gently. We must treat ourselves equally as gently. Having control of our emotions and thinking (or, in this case, writing) before we speak is an invaluable tool that can replace chaos with clarity and calm. I began to journal only recently. I look back at some of my own past mistakes and think how reactionary I was and wish I had someone to shove a pen in my hand and send me to the other room. Make the journal an extension of your body: go to the journal, use it, talk to it, throw it across the room if you must, receive comfort from it—whatever you need to do. Just make sure you go to your journal first before you say something you will later regret. I guarantee it will change the way you communicate with your partner and the way you express yourself in your life.

I also want you to use the journal when you are about to give too much information to your girl. You know what I mean by "too much information," don't you? Try to focus on the fact that your girlfriend isn't just your friend—she is your lover. Sure, she's a woman, she knows all about the horrors of monthly bloating and cramps. She has undoubtedly woken up with a hangover after puking the night before. She knows the pain of a yeast or urinary tract infection. But do you really need to discuss it with her in excruciating detail? No way, you have your journal now. Sharing information about feminine blahs is simply not sexy, though certainly understandable in conversation between two women. We must learn how to separate friend from girlfriend in some areas. If you simply must go into detail about what is the best douche to use, then call a friend. Spill your guts about the infection or about your cramps to this other lucky person or better yet, a journal that doesn't have a gag reflex. Have a blast, but don't bring that kind of talk into the bedroom. If it's something serious, then of course you will need to discuss it. Remember though that maintaining some mystery can do wonders. It's a small thing, but believe me, when we are trying to woo back our lover, we need all the help we can get. And talk of tampons, bloat or showing her the roll on our tummy that we wish we didn't have is simply not helpful. Re-train your mind and your dialogue when it comes to speaking to your lady. Words have power; let's use them to our advantage, shall we?

Your next assignment is to sit alone in a dark room by candlelight. Allow yourself to take a few deep-cleansing breaths. Look at yourself in the mirror and picture your relationship as perfect as it can be. Imagine your lover looking back at you with love in her eyes.

Imagine the two of you laughing together, holding each other and eventually making love. It may take quite a few tries to get to the point of picturing the two of you, bodies entwined, lost in a passionate embrace. It may simply be hard to imagine because it's hard to remember. That's ok. Take it slow. Then write about your wishes in your journal. Manifest them into being. Think about the way your lover looked at you the first time you pleasured her and saw her climax. Now FEEL it. Challenge yourself to really go back in time. Think about how warm her body felt, pressing up against your own skin. Remember how satisfied you were in that moment. Believe in your heart you will be there again. Say positive phrases out loud to give them power. Then, write them in your journal. For example, try saying something like " I see (insert your girlfriend or wife's name here) and I re-connecting in a spiritual and sexual way – it feels like butterflies in my belly" or "I see my girlfriend and myself re-establishing the intimacy that comes from touch and we are sexual beings drawn together by the Universe for the highest good. I feel her love. I feel her desire for me. I feel her heat and I am grateful." Then, return to present day. If you can, picture the two of you now, getting closer every day. Visualization can become a reality: if we can see it, it can be realized. Any doubts or visions of the two of you as strangers should be expelled from your mind. Just say "Delete" out loud or in your mind. Negative thoughts will bring you more negativity in your life. That was yesterday; today is a new day. Once you feel calm and certain that the two of you will again live as lovers, take a deep breath and begin to speak. Make a promise to yourself—aloud—that you will follow the plan in its entirety. Make a vow to yourself that even when you feel like the plan may not be working that you will stick it out.

Look down at your journal and see the power in writing in this book. Tell yourself that this month belongs to you and your girlfriend/wife and any other outside distractions will have to take a backseat to what you are trying to accomplish now. Make sure that you call in friends, family members or hired help to assist you with your children or companion animals. You must have dedicated time for each other this month. Remind yourself that you will stay the course, even when it's difficult, even when you doubt it will work. Then when you are feeling confident and peaceful, extinguish the candle. Repeat this ritual as necessary.

Congratulations, you are now taking an active role in changing the life you share with the woman of your dreams. Enjoy this moment- feel proud, strong and invincible. And, it's into the fire we go…

Chapter Five

Day 2- Cool Girlfriends Make Connections

Welcome to Day 2- today, we will discuss connections. I'd like to reference a little story that perfectly illustrates how important connecting is. Many years ago I saw a photo in one of the tabloids of Jennifer Lopez and Ben Affleck at an Oscar party. Jennifer looked gorgeous in a vintage Jackie Kennedy mint green gown. The photo showed her on the red carpet kissing Ben. Jennifer's eyes were almost closed, lost in the moment and Ben's were wide open looking at something past her shoulder. I remember shaking my head and thinking "they are not going to last". They broke up very soon after that photo appeared. It was clear that they weren't connecting.

When two lovers kiss they should either have their eyes closed, thinking about the kiss or be looking deeply into each other's eyes until the last second when their lips touch. Sharing a kiss is often more intimate than sharing bodily fluids. You absolutely must be present during this important moment. However, you may be thinking to yourself that you don't really kiss your woman all that often, if ever anymore, so we are getting a bit ahead of ourselves on Day 2. Don't worry; every exercise in this book will get your closer to lip locking and all that follows.

Let me remind you that connecting should not only be occurring when you are kissing. You should now make it a point to connect every time you are within a few feet of your girl. When she speaks to you, I want you to lock eyes with her. You will immediately feel the connection. You may be surprised by the energy that suddenly begins to pass between the two of you. It is downright electric when two women, who genuinely care about each other, lock eyes. It doesn't matter if all she is asking you is where she left her sunglasses or if the cat has been fed yet, lock eyes with her. You will probably see that she will be taken aback a bit by the intensity. It may even make the two of you slightly uncomfortable. That is fine—go with it. From this day forward whenever you are having a conversation with your woman, connect. It will immediately change the way you relate to each other and jump-start the ignition. It's an easy exercise to forget so do your best to remember. You may find that the first few times you won't even hear exactly what she is saying- you will probably be distracted by the intimacy of it. If that happens, rest assured you are doing the exercise properly. The only time you should not be locking eyes with her is when she is driving her car or shaving her legs (don't want any accidents there!). Otherwise, lock those eyes!

Then, choose a moment before or after dinner to use this exercise in a direct way. Introduce this exercise by saying something like "Babe, I read today about how important it is to connect. Can we sit here in silence together for just one minute locking eyes and see how we feel afterward?" Depending on where your relationship is she may think you are drunk or off your rocker—or she may feel immediately flattered and awestruck by your suggestion. If she agrees, put your phone on silent, put the kids to bed, turn off any distractions, give the dog or cat a toy to occupy themselves with and just sit in silence together.

Hold hands if it doesn't feel forced and breathe in slowly and in rhythm. If you laugh or look away at first that is ok. After a few seconds of the initial awkwardness it shouldn't be too difficult to carry out this exercise. You can set your alarm for one minute and have a go at it. After the exercise is completed share your feelings with her. It's ok to say it felt scary or weird. It's also ok to say it felt amazing to gaze at her that way. Then ask her how it felt for her. Whatever her response, provide a safe place for her to express to you her feelings. She may cry. She may have feelings of anger come up. She may find it easy or difficult. All of it is ok. Share the moment and accept each other unconditionally.

On the flip side, if she refuses to do the exercise for whatever reason let it go. It is not worth an argument. Just continue to lock eyes with her when you speak. That alone will provide a way in. Trust the process and release all blame. Perhaps later you can try for a longer time but for now we are starting off this process slow.

Chapter Six

Day 3- Cool Girlfriends Look Hot from Head to Toe

Think back to your first date with your lover. What did you wear? Did you have make up on? Jewelry? What did you wear to bed the first time you slept together? What kind of underwear did you have on? What kind of perfume? Did you get a manicure? Pedicure? Did you shave your legs? Did you shave or trim your pubic hair?

Chances are the answer to at least one of those questions is yes… And I would put money on the guess that it's more than one. Dare I ask how many of you can answer "yes" if I changed the question from "first date" to "last night"? How many of us have started out smelling good, looking great, and ended up wearing oversized old t-shirts to bed (not to say this can't be sexy but there's an oversized t-shirt and then there's the pink one with the cat on it our great aunt gave us for Christmas with holes in it), with a dab of acne medication on our chin? And then we end up wondering where the romance went. Duh!

Laziness can get to even the best of us but that is no excuse. In order to feel sexy, we have to believe we are sexy. And let me say right now you are beautiful. You are perfect. You don't have to change anything physically for a woman to love you. You don't have to look a certain way for a woman to want to have sex with you. I have fallen head over heels for people who don't look like supermodels. I don't personally care how many degrees you have or how book smart you are. But if something in the way you think sets you apart and makes you unique, I'm interested. If you live your life with passion, I am intrigued. If you live your life honestly and do not lie, I respect you. And if you can make me laugh, I am yours forever. Know who you are. Be proud of that woman. You are strong, you are invincible—you are woman. Now that I have gotten that very important message out of the way, it doesn't mean diddlysquat if YOU don't believe it. You must look in the mirror every day and say aloud, "I am beautiful just the way I am". Take ownership of how you look, how your inner beauty shines through your eyes. Your essence is conveyed by the way you walk, the way you behave, the way you glow. You are smokin'. Please live that feeling: Own it.

Believe it. Now, ask yourself "what do I have to do to make myself believe this truth?"

I remember being out to dinner once with someone who once meant a lot to me and I randomly asked her what she thought her most attractive body part was. She thought about it and said, "I don't have one, I don't think I am that attractive but I am smart." I remember that took my breath away. Not just because it was so honest, but she owned it. She didn't need validation on her physical appearance; she valued herself in other ways. She proved she was smart in her business and the way she took chances in her work. She had confidence in something that mattered to her and she worked it. I remember reaching out across the table for her hand without thinking. It was so sexy to hear that kind of honest confidence.

However, it is also true that the best revenge is looking good and living better. That has been incentive for a lot of people to hit the gym and look their best after a break up. Losing someone we love is hard and seeing them hook up with someone after the fact can make us feel self-conscious about our own image. Looks fade for everyone, but confidence can last a lifetime. If a woman has all of those qualities, that can seal the deal.

For some of us, if we take a hard look in the mirror we may see some things that require a few improvements in areas that we don't love about ourselves. That is understandable, but certainly don't get caught up in an illusion that you must look a certain way to be loved, especially by the woman who already shares your life and your bed. Nevertheless, do what you must to feel great in your body. Remember that it is self-confidence that we are after, not perfection. Sure, for some of us, that may require losing a few pounds. For others it's revamping our wardrobe. Some women get high looking at their hard six-pack abs or muscles. Some of us embrace our feminine curves—childbearing hips and all. Or for some of us, just feeling healthy and fit is enough. Go through your own body checklist and make whatever adjustments in your life that you feel comfortable making. LBD is something that manifests itself after a long time, during which many things also suffer. Our appearance can be one of them. So, let's get your fine self back into what I call the "first date flashback look".

Some of the things I am about to say may seem obvious. However, when we are in a relationship rut it is not uncommon for other aspects of our lives to fall into a rut as well. Again, trust me when I say its important that you read through all these suggestions and honestly ask yourself if you have "taken care" of this or that. Sometimes, we just get too comfortable and forget the little things. Sometimes, depression that stems from the lack of love we feel from our partner makes us feel too "tired" or "overwhelmed" to take care of the small details that are oh so important.

For example, I remember going through a break up with someone I was crazy about. It took everything I had just to get out of bed in the morning—let alone keep my career on track, get to the gym, take care of my animals, bring in the dry cleaning, go to the supermarket, etc. Then one day my friend asked me, "Simone, when was the last time you washed your hair?" Since I am a bit of a germaphobe and clean freak I had managed to take a steaming hot bath every morning, in which I would cry until the water went cold, but going the extra mile to wash my hair was just too much. It took her honesty to get me to take better care of myself. That is why I feel compelled to mention everything from your haircut to your nose hair in this chapter. Girlfriend, I've been there. I get it. Read on…

Simone Reyes

Your body- if you are comfortable with a few extra pounds then far be it for me to try to get you on a scale and on a diet. Some of my friends actually wear their extra pounds well and it adds to their look. Besides, a woman with a bit of meat on her bones offers more to hold onto. But if you don't feel fit, that's another thing. Don't overlook the plain fact that sex is a physical activity. It takes endurance and physical strength.

Sometimes you may want to hold difficult positions with your lover. Trying out different sexual positions will certainly require you to be able to hold your own body weight from time to time (whether you consider yourself more of a top girl or a bottom—and believe me I am going to have you in some interesting positions a few chapters forward, ladies!) Therefore, I highly recommend joining a gym, getting a trainer or at least setting aside an hour a day to pop in a yoga, Pilates, boxing or a hip hop dance class into your DVD player/ Apple TV to get your heart rate up. I guarantee you will feel sexier and be a better lover if you get your heart pumping at least three times a week. The endorphins that come from exercise and the act of getting your body moving is a natural aphrodisiac in itself. Use it.

Slaying the Lesbian Bed Death Dragon

If you smoke, try to cut down. I wouldn't recommend trying to quit this month, as there will be too much stress involved. If you decide to go cold turkey with such a powerful addiction, I worry that your journal will be filled with your fight against smoking and leave little time for dealing with relationship stuff. However, smoking will kill you and second hand smoke puts your family at risk. So please quit as soon as possible. If you drink too much, cut down. Excessive drinking in itself is usually a sign that there are issues you are trying to hide from in your relationship. If you eat too much junk, eat healthier. Distracting yourself with a temporary fix like food will only satisfy you while you eat and will ultimately make you unhappy and unhealthy. If you are a long time user of anti-depressants, ask your doctor if the dose needs to stay consistent or if you can try taking a lower dose. All of these things can help to get your libido back on track. Also, it's worth mentioning that seeing someone treat herself like they are worthy of getting love and attention is very sexy. Your body is a temple that your lover will be worshipping – treat it as such. It's a win /win situation all the way around. A body deserves to be adored and adorned.

Cool girlfriends know how to accessorize. Personally, when I see a chick wearing great sunglasses, she has already passed one of my initial tests. Wearing cool kicks also goes far for me. Come up with something that you love and treat yourself. You don't need to go into debt to buy some new accessories. When I want to treat myself I will often buy a great new lipstick or pair of pleather motorcycle boots—they don't break the bank, but they add flavor to an outfit. These are small things that can make an old outfit look like new. Maybe your new accessory will be a cool vintage ring or small stud earring that catches your eye. If you are a piercings girl, maybe switch them out and buy something new. Whatever you decide is your signature accessory, update that. And don't misunderstand; buying a new accessory will not impress your lover enough to make all of your problems disappear, but it will help you to look more polished and hopefully make you feel like you are treating yourself to something. Treating ourselves well shows our loved one that we take pride in ourselves, which is a very sexy attribute.

Grooming- Unless you are taking hormones and/or transitioning (or you and your lady have decided that you look best with some fuzz on your mug) there is no excuse for a uni-brow or a mustache. Some chicks dig a bit of facial hair on their partner; this is usually discussed early on so it shouldn't be a question at this point. However, if she doesn't and you are just being lazy, then get over to the local salon and book a lip waxing appointment and brow shaping. Eyebrows that are properly shaped can make you look more youthful, more awake and even highlight your cheekbones. I remember reading something that Elvis Presley once said about his co-star Ursula Andress- he said her cheekbones could cut glass. Maybe yours never will but why not do what you can to bring them out. On the flip side, eyebrows that look like worms look terrible. Don't over-pluck either or they may not grow back. You can easily deal with your mustache by either going to the drugstore and purchasing an over the counter bleaching kit or book an appointment to get it waxed/threaded at a salon.

And please don't neglect nose hair. Nobody enjoys seeing that! Even the most hard-core stone butch who likes a bit of facial hair on her face should never ever be seen with nose hair popping out to say hello to the world. Get a nose hair clipper and go to town. Please! Personal grooming shows that we respect our bodies—and respect for ourselves elicits respect from our loved one. Simple.

Skin- Lord, if we could all have pore-less looking skin like Jennifer Lopez or Gisele Bundchen then we would never have to worry about how we look in the cold light of day ever again. However, beautiful skin takes work for most. If you don't get regular facials or micro-dermabrasion what are you waiting for? Although it is scientifically proven that the use of some oral contraceptives can cut down on adult acne breakouts there are other options available. Sometimes just finding a great facialist is an easier (and many will argue, a safer) alternative to taking medications. There is also some evidence that oral contraceptives may decrease libido so that's an even better reason to try to treat bad skin with a good facialist. Bad skin at any age takes a huge toll on one's self-confidence. In fact, people who suffered from teenage acne are often so scarred by it emotionally that even when their skin is clear, they may feel self-conscious about it. Remember, we don't need to be perfect to win our lover back, we just need to take good care of ourselves and take ownership of the fact that we are all beautiful in our own way.

You must do what you can to feel good in your own skin. Now for the skin on your body, be sure to use a loofa brush to scrub away dead skin. Bring body scrubs into the shower and scrub away. You want her hands to feel your soft, silky skin, don't you? When you get out of the bath, moisturize your body with a scent you love.

These small indulgences will make you feel sexy, I promise. Since we are at it, why not try some shimmer on your stomach, arms and shoulders? If you have been working out, it will give a hint of va va voom to those glistening muscles. If not, the shimmer will look pretty and will be an unexpected treat for your girl to feast her eyes on.

Make up- Some of our more tomboy sisters shun makeup. Most seem to like a clean face. I do as well, however, when we are in the fight of our lives to win back our lover, sometimes we have to bring out the big guns. I would never suggest full foundation, eye shadow, and mascara for everyday. It looks like you are trying much too hard. For example, when I watch *The Real Housewives of Beverly Hills,* (I love to binge on those shows as much as anybody) I am so disappointed in how much make-up those women cake on their face. Besides, putting on too much make up is a sign of insecurity. And while common, insecurity should never be flown like pride flag. We all tend to fly our freak flags soon enough anyway, let's not add that one to our parade. That said, when you do go out for a night on the town with your girl, a bit of concealer goes a long way. Cover up any pigment issues on your face, erase under eye circles, etc. Make sure to test the concealer in daylight when you purchase it- an ill matching one will look awful. A hint of blush and lip-gloss can really brighten up your look without employing full war paint. I highly recommend just a bit of color on your face; it can do wonders.

Tanning- there is no better way to glow than to bronze a bit. Now we don't have to worry about skin cancer anymore; all we have to do is go to one of those spray on tanning places, put on a shower cap, close our eyes and get golden. I highly recommend this. Not only does a tan make you appear thinner, but also it just seems to make everyone look more alive. Do be careful to apply some creamy Vaseline to your elbows, hands and feet, as they do tend to get blotchy from the spray.

Tats- Oh, how I love tattoos. I love the way they look, I love the way they move on a well-toned arm, I love to hear the stories of why, where and how they were acquired (unless, of course, their significance involves a past love.) If you have a tattoo of an ex girlfriend's name/her initial/her astrological sign, etc. that you just haven't gotten around to getting rid of, do it. How long did Johnny Depp, Heidi Klum or Angelina Jolie hold on to their tattoos of Winona, Seal or Billy Bob—not for long. Who cares that your ex is never a thought? Who cares if you left her on the worst possible terms? Who cares that she's straight now and married with five kids? It's disrespectful and a real passion killer to have your woman seeing that on a daily basis. Bite the bullet and get rid of it. Now!

While I would never dare to tell you hopelessly romantic ladies not to get a tattoo of your girlfriend on your body, this can often backfire in more ways than one. Yes, the obvious backfire is that you break up/get divorced and have to get it removed or made into a flower or something, but also consider that some women may feel that having her name on your body adds pressure to the union. You never know how a woman is going to react to such a surprise so before doing anything so permanent, please discuss it with your chick first. And then reconsider.

Mani/Pedi- Yes, we all know for obvious reasons the importance of keeping our fingernails short. Nothing kills the mood like an ouch down below. However, that is no reason to keep them sloppy. Whether you prefer them natural or painted fire engine red they should be professionally manicured. That goes for toes as well. Let's proudly own the title "fiddlers" by showing the world how lovely (and skillful) lesbian fingers are.

Simone Reyes

Personally, I can tell a lot about someone just by looking at her hands. And I am not referring to the "scientists from California finding that lesbian women have a greater difference in length between their ring finger and index finger than straight women do" thing. Fingernails should always be clean and well taken care of. Your hands will soon re-gain access to your girlfriends sacred place, so they simply must look worthy enough to pass through the velvet rope.

Hygiene- there is no mood buster worse than halitosis. Of course, there are often overlooked causes for not having your breath smell right. Perhaps you are getting sick or you just ate something seasoned with onions or garlic, etc., but always do your part and carry mints or gum with you. If you can't find a mint, an apple is often helpful. Never miss your dental appointments and get your teeth cleaned regularly. Buy a tongue cleaner. The tongue can hold a lot of foul-smelling bacteria, especially towards the back. You may never make a better two-dollar investment than a tongue cleaner.

Floss every day. Foods trapped between teeth make your mouth into a garbage disposal. And finally, whiten those teeth. Go to the local drugstore and purchase some whitening strips. And for all you really lazy gals, if you have the cash, you can always book a professional whitening at your dentist's office. It takes about an hour or so and you can literally see your teeth a few shades lighter as soon as you leave the facility. However, afterward you may feel some tooth sensitivity and you will be told, for a time, only to eat white foods. Hey, it's an excuse to eat a lot of mashed potatoes. Yum.

Feminine Hygiene- Even the gold-est star lesbian can be turned off by normal feminine bodily smells, an odor after menstruation or a natural female scent that is too strong. Let's face it, when LBD is sleeping in our beds, almost any excuse not to go down is employed. But there is good news ahead! Many feminine hygiene manufacturers sell small packets that you can easily carry in your pocket or wallet that help a woman feel and smell fresh. During our monthly cycle it is lovely to have a small wipe to keep the area clean and smelling nice. Your woman will appreciate that you are going that extra mile to be as alluring as possible.

Deodorants- This issue can be debatable. One of my friends goes absolutely insane by the scent of her girlfriend's perspiration. She finds it very erotic and pleasing. They often have sex right after her lady comes back from jogging. I say, more power to them. But, from my experience my friend is definitely in the minority. The smell of sweat doesn't turn me on, so I am a fan of deodorant. It's your call ladies but I say better safe than sorry; keep some deodorant on hand at all times. I prefer the natural crystal rock variety; I don't like chemicals that close to my lymph nodes.

Hair- In a study entitled "First Impressions and Hair Impressions," conducted by Dr. Marianne LaFrance, a Gender Studies Professor at Yale, the way you wear your hair creates an immediate and long-lasting effect on people you meet. Long gone are the days where lesbians were identified by mullets and buzz cuts. Whatever your preference—long, short, flipped, Yuko-ed or shaggy—make sure you get a great cut and keep it conditioned. Hair should look shiny, healthy and alive. Maybe you like your grey- if you do, rock it. If not and you are just lazy, then cover it up. Play with different colors; it may be fun to try being a brunette for a month or go platinum. You only live once! And try a hair mask once a month. You want your lover to run her fingers through it, don't you? If your look is outdated go to a great salon and have them give you a makeover. Get rid of those split ends and don't go about your day with bed head. Take a few extra moments to style it in the mornings so that your lover will see you at your best every day going forward. I also think caps and baseball hats look very sexy on a woman. Experiment with different looks. And always have a cap on hand when you are having a bad hair day- better to hide it than flaunt it.

Chapter Seven

Day 4- Cool Girlfriends Look Ultra- Sexy "Down There"

Feeling sexy is different for all of us. Personal turn-ons vary with each individual. When it comes to pubic hair, some women get turned on by seeing a full bush. Others prefer no hair at all and some get really hot by witnessing nothing short of an art show down below. By now I assume you know what your lover likes and there is no shame in admitting that when the fire started burning on low that you made fewer visits to the waxing salon. Your assignment is to switch it up. If you haven't ever gotten a bikini wax now is the time to try it out. Why not get creative? Why not visit Brazil?

The Brazilian Bikini Wax! Oh so popular and oh so lovely. There are a few variations on this waxing procedure when it comes to how much (if any) pubic hair you want to keep above/on the lips of your vagina. However, the overall theme of getting a Brazilian wax is that less is more. Once a woman goes Brazilian she almost never goes back. And I am not just talking about the person getting the Brazilian wax, if you catch my drift. It is one of the easiest things we can do for our lover that she is (most likely) guaranteed to love. Did I say easy? Well, ok that is a bit of an exaggeration unless you think getting a pap smear is a walk in the park. For those of you who have never had a Brazilian wax I will say this, it's like getting a pap smear but takes about six to ten minutes longer, is much more embarrassing, entails getting into a whole lot of mortifying positions and it hurts like hell. BUT your lover is worth it, right? Right. And the payback for both of you is worth every minute of torture.

Still not convinced? Still wondering what the big deal is?

Well, first of all, you will never feel so clean. Seeing your private area so exposed is liberating. You will soon realize that having this kind of wax reminds you of sex every time you go into the bathroom, every time you shower, every time you change your clothes. It puts sex on the brain- a very good thing to cure the LBD syndrome. There is an old episode of "Sex and the City" where all the girls get Brazilian waxes while on vacation in Los Angeles. When Carrie finds herself alone with a man she barely knows she goes with her feelings, explaining that the "Brazilian made me kiss him". From your lover's point of view, there is nothing better to find when she gets down there than a little surprise that says you have taken the time to groom for her pleasure.

The Brazilian is a gift to her and she knows it. It's naughty at its naughtiest. And the best part is its smooth. It makes oral sex an incredibly sensual event that allows your lover to see everything up close.

Some women opt for the removal of all bikini hair, which means everything from front to back (labia and butt included) is waxed. This is extremely popular right now. Some go for having their panty line sides waxed into a "V" or a straight line. Some enjoy having the panty line waxed, the butt waxed and leaving the labia not waxed. Some ladies prefer to leave a thin line, often referred to as a "landing strip" left on top with the strip of hair remaining down the lips. Another option is to leave just a small quarter sized ball of hair while taking off hair from the labia and the butt. Then of course for special occasions waxing salons often offer dying of pubic hair, plucking to create a design in your lover's initial or adorning the area with stick- on crystals. The options are endless! Remember, sex is supposed to be fun. A good and creative wax can also help you enjoy every luscious move she tries on you. The only downside, as I stated earlier, is you will now have to keep up "private appearances" every few weeks. Personally, I prefer going and having mine waxed by a professional (it's the masochist in me no doubt) but there is nothing wrong with carefully (emphasis on carefully ladies, please!) using a razor to keep that clean shave. Or invest in a Brazilian laser package.

I will leave it up to you to decide which waxing style to choose, but I encourage you strongly to try something new and/or different with your pubes. I promise you the effort will be worth it whether you decide to keep up with it or not.

Your lover will thank you over and over again. A Brazilian is the gift that literally keeps on giving and giving and giving. Think of it as the energizer pussycat. And on the off chance you don't absolutely love it, it's hair for goodness sakes… it will grow back!

Chapter Eight

Day 5-Cool Girlfriends Give Compliments- and Clues of What's To Come

This chapter, dear sisters, is the chapter where we set the stage for our future. It isn't smart to suddenly become someone else in a relationship, even if the "someone else" is a more improved version of who we are. Therefore, it's important to clue in our lover and let them know that we are aware that the relationship is in trouble and that we are going to try to do our part to bring the passion back. Never make her feel that LBD is her fault, nor is it necessary for you to blame yourself. LBD is usually a product of circumstance and it is seldom anyone's fault. Besides, blame never heals anything.

Start the day off by having a private moment of reflection by yourself. Listen quietly to your inner voice as you reflect on what you are grateful. If you meditate, even better. Ground yourself and keep an open mind and heart.

Slaying the Lesbian Bed Death Dragon

Now for the exercise. This is the day to talk about that elephant in the room. Please remember to tread lightly and always be cautious when bringing up your sex life—or lack of frequent sex, I should say. You should begin this exercise by setting aside a moment today where you begin to have a serious talk with your woman. Let your girlfriend know how important she is in your life and how much you want to love her better. The conversation needn't be long or particularly uncomfortable for that matter. Sometimes a one-liner is good enough. Consider saying something like, "Honey, I've been thinking about all the things I should feel grateful for instead of focusing on what I don't have or what I wish was better. I just want you to know I am so grateful you are in my life and I have decided to remember that gratefulness every day". You should feel free to phrase this sentiment any way you feel most comfortable expressing it. The point is to tell her in no uncertain terms that she is important to you and that you are going to make a conscious effort to let her see, feel and honor that every day.

This short conversation may open itself up to something much larger. If it does go deeper try to keep your emotions in check. Do your best to guide it away from any kind of argument. Sometimes when people feel moved by something their partner says it opens up a Pandora's box of emotions they have locked away. Sometimes it causes a flood of tears. Sometimes the tears are happy and sometimes they are sad. Sometimes these emotions are filled with pain and even anger. If the talk gets too heavy, you can always just tell her you love her and leave it at that until things calm down.

If you are both feeling open and honest, it may give way to a deeper understanding and safe place for the two of you to discuss your relationship. Whatever the outcome, keep your journal handy; you may need it now more than ever. In the best of outcomes, she will feel your hopefulness and respond with an open and warm heart. However, be prepared for anything and take it as it comes. Remember, LBD took a long time to get its hooks into you and your partner, so don't be surprised if it takes a long time to get it out of your life. Finish the conversation by saying "If I seem to be a bit different going forward it is because I want to come from a place of gratitude for having you as my girl". This will cue her into your intentions and soften her heart. I guarantee it.

Then make it a point to remind her (not just today but every day) why you fell in love with her. Be specific when you pay her a compliment. Don't just say " This dessert is good, babe". Instead consider saying " This dessert shows you put a lot of time and energy into baking it. It's delicious, thank you". Never wait for her to ask you how she looks. Whether she just woke up or spent an hour getting ready for an event, tell her how beautiful she is. Instead of saying " You look great," consider saying "You have the fullest lips, that's just another reason why kissing you will always be better than kissing anyone else." Be flirty. If she walks past you wearing jeans that make her ass look amazing, give it a little smack. Tell her she looks amazing in those jeans. She will love the extra attention. If she says something endearing take the time to say, "You are so cute right now". Everyone loves a compliment however big or small. Don't ever force a compliment. Be open to truly seeing your woman. From there the sweet words should flow naturally. Once you begin to articulate what you find hot about her don't stop there. Don't be stingy with them. Say them often when the moment strikes you. Use your wit to charm the pants off of her… literally!

Chapter Nine

Day 6- Cool Girlfriends Leave Hidden Notes

Do you remember when we were little shorties in school passing notes around? It was so worth risking detention for! There was just something so naughty and fun about passing those notes behind the teacher's back, it was impossible not to take the risk. Usually I would get some silly note from a friend that just wanted to know what I was having for lunch that day or a little joke about this or that. But sometimes the note came from a secret admirer or someone I had a crush on. Those notes were special and I will always remember them. Today, I suppose text messaging and emails have taken the place of little notes. What a shame—by which I mean you can't exactly fold up a text screenshot, make it look like a plane and send it flying across a classroom. Ah, those were the days.

So, my assignment for you today is to write a few notes to your girl and hide them in places she won't expect to find them. You can hide them in her briefcase, wallet, jeans pocket—even pinned inside her bra! These notes don't have to be long. In fact, they should be quite short. They should say things like, "I miss you," "I love you," "I can't wait 'til I can hold you tonight," etc. Leaving little notes is *trés romantique* and goes with the charm of old school courting. Personally, I can't think of a sweeter gesture. It will probably make your woman feel like a schoolgirl again. Don't be surprised if you get a call immediately from her telling you how you made her day. She will think of this gesture frequently and it will make her swoon just a little. It will also help her see you as a romantic partner again rather than her buddy/roommate. And try to stay clear of sending these notes via email or text message. I want you to really show some effort—texting is just too easy. Let her see your handwriting. Let her find the note somewhere unexpected. Make the effort!

Off you go now. Head on out to the store to buy your little note paper. And why not spritz it with your favorite scent. Let's go all out; she deserves it! And while we are on the subject of scent, if you don't have a signature scent I suggest you consider getting one. When she recognizes it on you it will make her feel like home.

Chapter Ten

Day 7- Cool Girlfriends Flirt (But Save The Last Dance for Their Woman)

If ever you needed your journal, tonight will be the night. This homework is a bit risky because it involves the green-eyed monster: jealousy. Caution must be exercised if this assignment is to be successful. Make a date with your partner to meet at a girl bar with friends. Tell her you want to "pick her up". Explain that you think it will be exciting to go separately, to talk to other women, even flirt (a little!) and then know without a shadow of a doubt that you both will be going home together. If she seems nervous about the prospect, tell her you are having the same feelings but that ultimately, it will be a real turn on to pick up a stranger AKA her.

Tell her you have been reminiscing in your mind about the first time you saw her. Maybe you knew the instant you spotted her across a crowded room that she was the one. Maybe it happened organically as friends and blossomed into not being able to sit next to each other without touching. Tell her you want to recreate that feeling.

Give each other clear permission to engage in conversation with other women: You are both even allowed to flirt a tiny bit, but NO TOUCHING IS ALLOWED. That means no leaning in too close, no putting your hand on a girl's knee when speaking, no dancing, nothing. All you are allowed to do is talk to another girl if the opportunity presents itself. Don't lead anyone on either, but remember that socializing is still legal here.

Keep in mind, that we always want what someone else wants—that's just the way nature works. That is also why we often see separated couples getting back together when a new love interest steps in. However, jealousy is not love and these relationships often fall apart later when the chase ends. This exercise will allow you both to understand that you are each desirable to other women and that you are both lucky to have found each other.

Now you may be thinking it's quite early in the plan for this exercise. It's not. While on one hand I don't want you to rush the process, I do want you to be fully committed to this plan. I want your partner to be receptive. This exercise, while innocent, does open up some pretty big what ifs. What if she thinks that girl is cooler than me? What if that girl she dated who still has a thing for her is there and she realizes she is interested? What if she sees I am not the only fish in the sea? Scary thoughts, yes, but oh so necessary. Have faith. This is all part of the big plan.

Let's begin! Agree to go to the gay bar at the same time but separately. Each of you should go with another friend in separate cars. Once inside, mingle with other women, but do NOT touch anyone. Try to fight the urge to stare at your partner to see what she is doing and with whom. Of course it's natural to want to glance over at her but if you spend all night staring at each other you won't be doing the exercise properly.

Order a drink (just one, let's not get sloppy ladies), dance and enjoy the night. Engage other women and be friendly. If you suspect another patron thinks you are there to pick them up, tell them that you are in a committed relationship but out with some friends tonight. After about an hour, approach your girlfriend. Ask her what her name is and if you may buy her a drink (this is drink number two and you are both now officially cut off). Ask her where she is from, if she is having a good night, etc. If there is a dance floor ask her to dance. Woo her. Interact with her like it is the very first time you have ever met. Stop yourself from touching her in any familiar way (it would be inappropriate to grab at a stranger). Continue to get to know your woman tonight, maybe you will find out something new about her.

    Be aware that you are in a room with other women who are most likely all there to meet someone special. If you weren't with your partner, chances are she would be making a connection with someone else tonight. Think about how that thought makes you feel. Maybe you and her are both feeling pangs of jealousy or insecurity. If so, good! It's a bit of a wake up call to realize that if you weren't in the picture, there will always be some other woman waiting in the wings to take your place. Really think about that. That realization is both a blessing and a warning. If relationships aren't meant to last it's good to know that there are other people who will be waiting in the wings for both of you. If you are sure you are with your partner out of genuine true love with a partnership built on trust, then this evening should be respectful and eye opening. Write about it in your journal tonight and thank the heavens you are the one who will get this beautiful creature to go home with you.

It is worth mentioning that partnerships and marriages don't mean you own another person. It is a promise, a vow. However, at the end of the day we can never control what another person does, even if it is something that is hurtful. All we can do is treat her the way we want to be treated and assume, if we choose our partner correctly, the same respect will be returned.

Then, once you are both ready to leave the club or bar, ask her if you can drive her home. Once at your place, walk her to the door and ask if you can come inside. Maybe the night will end with just a kiss goodnight as you laugh about it later or perhaps you will make love, touching each other as if her body is virgin territory. It's all up to you both.

This may be a good time to address the spice up tip that you may have read if googling for ideas on revving up your sex life : The Threesome. You may have thought about this fantasy from time to time. Perhaps you have heard from your girlfriend/wife that she would be open to having a third party join you both in the sack. This may be the section of the book where I show my conservative side, but lesbian bed death is a serious issue, whether or not you decide to label it LBD or not. Yes, I am providing many fun and interesting ways to tackle it, but we must never take our eye off the ball. And having a night with a stranger or a friend (male or female) can be fun at the time, but I wouldn't jump on that plan so fast, my friend! What you and your woman do behind closed doors is nobody's business but I feel obligated to caution you if her desires (or yours for that matter) involve the following: inviting a friend into the bedroom, hiring a hooker, having a male over for a threesome, etc. You get what I am saying.

Many of these fantasies are common but there is a difference between fantasy and reality. I certainly agree that two women should have enough trust between them to share every fantasy but I can't say that I would encourage any of the threesome fantasies to become a reality without serious consideration. This being especially true when we are right in the middle of fighting off LBD. I realize that threesomes are popular with many couples and I'm sure that some are able to do this without having it impact their relationship in a negative way. That said, in my own experience, I have seldom seen women sharing their girlfriend with someone else lead to anything positive.

Even if in your mind you get turned on thinking of your mate having sex with someone else, actually seeing it live and in person is another thing entirely. Some fantasies are best left in the brain. Jealousy and insecurity are powerful emotions. Therefore, allowing a stranger or even a trusted friend into your bedroom is a risk of mammoth proportions. What if either one of you likes having sex with this friend just a bit too much? Or what if it just looks to you like she does? Will you assume—correctly or incorrectly—that every time you are pleasuring her and her eyes are closed, that she is thinking about your mutual friend? Probably. What about the male stranger you both decide to pick up at a club? Do you suddenly fear that your strap-on can't compete with his real penis? Maybe. Maybe not. What I am trying to say is IF you take the risk of inviting someone else into your special space, you better be sure you are both prepared to handle the feelings that it may elicit. Not a whole lot of them are pretty.

If you want to go down that road, be prepared to deal with the consequences. Lesbian Bed Death is a serious issue and throwing another body into the mix is just going to complicate things in my opinion. If you do decide to go ahead with that kind of a fantasy please do

Slaying the Lesbian Bed Death Dragon

so responsibly and safely. That is all I will say on the subject.

Chapter Eleven

Day 8- Cool Girlfriends Spoil Their Woman Good

Once upon a time I met someone who seemed perfect for me. I will save you the long, sad, tragic story and simply say that it didn't work out. Actually, it quite mysteriously ended almost as soon as it began. It still bothers me to this day. Recently it came up in conversation with a friend and I said, "You know the worst part is that she never really got to know me, never got to experience the part of me that was going to treat her unlike any woman before me or after me for that matter."

I felt so instantly connected to this woman that instead of thinking about all the things the relationship was going to do for me, and how happy she was going to make me—I was totally excited about all the great, cool and unique things I had in store for her. I knew that we would have been the most talked about power couple in town. I knew we would have been perfection. Instead of seeing that part of me, she only ultimately got to see the worst—a frustrated and angry child who was faced with someone missing out on the best thing ever. Unfortunately for both of us she would never know how good it could have been if she didn't self-sabotage. If that relationship had been given a chance and she turned out to be the woman of my dreams, I would have indulged her every fantasy. I would have let her shine and show her off like the diamond I believed her to be. I know I would have been someone she never would be able to get out of her mind or her heart because I would have showed up for her. That is what I am trying to show you how to do. I can't help but think about a line from one of my all time favorite songs by Stevie Nicks. In her song, "Silver Springs" she sings, "I know I could have loved you but you would not let me."

Let's picture for a moment what this woman would have been rewarded with if she had let me love her. When she came home after a long day at work, I would be waiting at the door of our house that smelled heavenly, wearing something casually hot, holding a cold drink for her. I would have drawn her a bath, put on her favorite music, researched a movie that she has been interested in seeing and made love to her in a different ways every night of her life. I know what you are thinking, that chick missed out, right? Tru dat! I would never write a book about being the coolest girlfriend if I didn't know how to be just that. That isn't ego, darling—it's training.

Well, ladies, take a cue from me, spoiling a woman is the most fun you can have out of bed and she will be floored by it as well. Who wouldn't? Now, I am not talking about being a slave. Do not get it confused. Cleaning up after someone, being their punching bag and losing yourself is not love and it certainly isn't sexy. If only one person is behaving in this Queen role, then this is not a good match. Spoiling is a two way street. It is fine to initiate these special evenings, but they must be reciprocated. Respect is earned. Don't ever be a doormat and don't ever treat your partner as one.

Don't ever be a secret. A woman who has truly met her match screams about you from the rooftops. She is so proud to have you on her arm, her Instagram and Facebook is flooded with photos of the two of you together. She believes she has won the jackpot. She believes that you have the most class, the hottest body and the most intelligent wit she has ever encountered—even if you don't! That is what you deserve. So does she if she is the one. So, draw her that bath, wake her up with breakfast in bed, cook her a delicious dinner, rub her feet while she watches television, walk the dog when she is tired, clean out the kitty litter before she gets to it, give her a massage, wear your hair the way she likes it, contribute financially and equally to the union, make her proud to show you off etc. Basically, think of all the things you wish someone would do for you and then do them for her. Don't take her for granted for one more day!

One of the most unexpected places to pamper someone is on an airplane. The next time you take a trip together pack a few of her favorite snacks as a surprise and present them when you reach cruising altitude. Ask the attendant for a blanket and get her hot at 35,000 feet.? The Mile High Club is one we should all join. It's easy to drape a blanket over the two of you during a night flight and to slip your hand down her jeans. Finger her under the blanket when nobody is watching. This is especially good for a red eye flight when the lights are turned down anyway. Then when the two of you can't stand it anymore quietly disappear into the tiny bathroom and go down on her (more on this later) or continue pleasing her with your fingers. Make it a flight she will always remember. Ok, so the tiny bathroom with the florescent lighting isn't exactly the most romantic spot in the world but sometimes doing a quick sexual act somewhere completely out of your familiar territory is very, very hot. At this point you may be saying, "when is it my turn?" Patience, dear girl. Unless your girlfriend is the most selfish woman on the planet, she will reciprocate your loving gestures. It may take a while, but she will. What we give, we get. Your chance will come, but for now, concentrate on spoiling that woman good. Seeing the pleasure in her face will be enough for now. We have only just begun.

Chapter Twelve

Day 9- Cool Girlfriends Know How to Prep a Room For Seduction

Think of a few words to describe your bedroom. If they don't contain the adjectives inviting, romantic, cozy, sensual, sexy and luxurious, then your boudoir needs a makeover. Let's start with lighting. Bright lights invite inhibition into your sacred place and do little to help you unwind at the end of a hard day. Not to mention, everyone looks better in a room that comes with a dimmer switch! Colored light bulbs can create different atmospheres and invoke many different feelings. Blue bulbs create a space that seems mysterious, pink bulbs feel warm and romantic, red bulbs scream sex and there is nothing wrong with that! Black lights are a bit scary (best saved up for Halloween) same for green and yellow.

My all time favorite way to create romantic mood lighting is with scented candles, incense and firelight. Just the crackling of a fire makes me think of getting cozy with a loved one. One word of caution, once you start to buy enough candles to light a church, make sure you keep them away from drafts and in secure candle holders—the fire you start must remain in your pants, not in your home!

Let's talk about your bed. I would never suggest that you buy a new bed immediately but if you aren't absolutely in love with the one you have, it is a wonderful and practical investment. Make sure your mattress and box spring are suited to both of your preferences. In terms of comfort, here's a little tip Brad Pitt has been known to pass around: don't waste your money on a big giant quilted expensive mattress. Instead, purchase a firm mattress and add on a three-inch Tempur-Pedic pad memory foam. Apparently this works for Brangelina- so it's good enough for me (smile). Actually, I sleep in a canopy bed that is draped in gauze-like curtains so that when I desire, I can draw them around me and make the world disappear. I often hang white Christmas or fairy lights around the bed to add a kind of enchanted cottage feel.

Hey, it's worth pointing out that the bigger the bed the more room there is for play—so if you do decide to invest in a new bed, why not make it a king size? You both deserve the best. Since we are on the topic of beds, bedding is ultra important. Go out and buy some really great linen with a high thread count. If you are feeling really sex kittenish, why not try some satin sheets? It's a cool, slinky, awesome feeling when you slide around on satin sheets. Think of it like a Slip n' Slide. It's impossible not to think about sex when you are rolling around on satin sheets.

Flowers can add a lovely touch to a room so consider placing some on your night table. There is nothing more lovely than a beautiful bouquet of flowers to set a romantic tone in your bedroom. And while on the subject of bedrooms, let us not forget how vital the right music playlist is for setting the mood.

Music is possibly the most important ingredient for setting the stage for seduction. Make a playlist that you know your woman loves of the most romantic songs you can think of. Remember to choose songs that are sexy. Personally, I could listen to the haunting voice of Stevie Nicks and the pop songs of Pink forever but neither of them would be my first choice to make love to. Instead, I gravitate more toward a mix of Leonard Cohen, Lorde, Tegan and Sara, Phoenix, Beyonce or when I am feeling really naughty, David Banner. What I am trying to say is, understand the difference and make a playlist based on songs you both love and will feel turned on by.

Make sure you buy some massage oils and keep them near the bed for an impromptu massage. Essential oils have been touted to have aphrodisiac powers, so why not try some behind your ear? Lavender, rose, ylang-ylang and jasmine are all recommended by the pros. Please make sure that all essential oils are companion animal-friendly if you share your home with little ones. We all know how important our companion animals are!

And while you are out purchase some lubricant. Lube is another good thing to have around, especially when we get to our sex toys section. Now that I just used the word "toys," don't be tempted to jump ahead. Rushing her won't work; we must stay on course.

Of course, make sure your kitchen is always stocked with her favorite refreshments—beer, wine, tequila, Champagne, spring water or green juice—whatever she likes to indulge in. Your home is your sanctuary. It is often the little things that mean the most. Knowing that your woman is thinking of you when she is out running errands, stopping off at the grocery store, buying little things and hiding them to surprise you with over the holidays all mean that you are a priority. Everyone wants to feel special. We give what we get. Good givers are great getters. So, give a little more than you have before and just watch the unfolding of it being returned.

Simone Reyes

Chapter Thirteen

Day 10- Cool Girlfriends Dig The Spook

Studies have indicated that there is evidence to support that anxiety-producing situations create a more erotic turn-on. Don't worry I am not suggesting you tie yourself to a train track and have your girlfriend rescue you as the train approaches. I'm just going to send you to the movies to catch a horror flick. A movie theater is the perfect place to explore a small degree of touching and intimacy in a public place—just to get your feet wet. Plus, the thrill of feeling scared is going to add to the fun.

Make sure the movie you choose is considered to be REALLY scary—one that will get your heart racing. Note: I said scary, not gory… you don't want to make your girl ill. I happen to love horror movies but I have dated some who aren't as enthusiastic. If she needs a little enticement remind her that it's all just an excuse to sit close to her. She will love to hear that. And yes, you will both instinctively sit closer to each other, grab for each other and bury your head in each others lap as the movie gets more terrifying. Perfect. Now, if you simply cannot wait to hold each other… hey, it's a dark theater, why not make out right there? Sit in the back row and think back to your first dates with your girlfriend. Relive those feelings all over again. And don't be surprised if the two of you sleep even closer together tonight fearing a visit from the boogeyman!

Or go skydiving! If you haven't jumped out of a plane why not consider taking the plunge? This terrifying activity is sure to make memories that last a lifetime with the one you hope to spend the rest of your life with.

For those who aren't convinced about jumping out of a plane why not consider trapeze class? I loved taking trapeze, but climbing up to that height, holding onto a bar swinging upside down and then letting go wasn't a cakewalk—it was terrifying (safety harness or not!) In these kinds of situations, if you are in a small group of strangers learning how to face your fear, you will probably feel at least a slight bonding towards these people from your shared experience. Imagine how bonded you will feel with your girlfriend or wife.

Simone Reyes

Go online and find something that terrifies you, make a date with your girl and go for it! Buckle up!

Chapter Fourteen

Day 11- Cool Girlfriend's Kiss Their Woman as if She is Going Off to War

Nothing compares to the first kiss. Even if it was sloppy, quick, or interrupted, it was still the best. And no, you won't ever be able to recapture that feeling ever again, but you can come close. Sure, it won't ever be as mystical, magical, scary, unfamiliar, exciting, unexpected and wondrous as the first time she kissed you. Maybe you won't be able to feel her trembling under your hand or hear your own heartbeat through your shirt. Maybe you won't feel flushed and nervous. That special moment only happens once. However, you can still make her weak in the knees if you lay one on her when she least expects it. Make sure you pop in a mint first and smell great. Be sure your movements are fluid and well rehearsed. Wait until she is lost in some mundane task i.e. doing the laundry, cooking, cleaning, reading, etc. Then, sneak up behind her and slowly spin her around. Don't go right in for the kiss. A kiss should never feel aggressive or forced. There is nothing worse than a tongue being thrust into your mouth when you aren't in the mood. Go slow and yet keep up a steady pace.

Let me explain: turn your woman around, put your hand on her head and brush away some hair from around her face. Look into her eyes for about a second, and drop your hand behind her neck. Then take your other hand and put that on the other side of her head so that you have some control of how her head tilts. Gently kiss her. Supporting her head, stop and look into her eyes and then go in again. Do not use tongue at this point. Look at her again in the eye and then go in with a slight, gentle bit of tongue. Guide her head with your hands. This should not be a kiss that is meant to lead to sex. If it does, terrific but do not put your hands on her breasts, even if you want to. Do not go near her genital area, although you may start to feel hot down there. Just focus on her and her eyes. Then walk away.

The next morning when she is heading off to work you are going to repeat exactly the same move but there will be a different finish thrown in. After you separate, after you have given her the real kiss, allow your hand that is currently behind her head to drop down past her shoulder and let it gently and slowly graze the side of her breast. Then tell her to have a great day and that you will be thinking of her until she gets home. Believe me that kiss, coupled with that surprise lingering touch will replay over and over again during the course of her day, not only because she will be thinking of where else you will be kissing her later but because she really, truly knows you desire her.

Once we have really blasted that bed death dragon out of the water, long after this thirty-day guide, I want you to start every day with a knock-her-socks-off kiss. Like the chapter heading says, kiss her like she is going off to war. Kiss her like you may never see her again. Kiss her like she is going boxing with Ronda Rousey—oh, the horror! Kiss her like you mean it. If you do, she will never stray from you. She will be yours forever. Like so many song lyrics say, it's all in the kiss.

Chapter Fifteen

Day 12- Cool Girlfriends Send Flowers

Ah, old school courting—it will make any woman weak. I vividly remember the first time a woman sent me flowers. They arrived via FedEx early on a Saturday morning, laying flat in a large rectangular box. I knew who sent them as soon as the doorbell rang. For some reason, all the giant flower arrangements I had ever received from men paled in comparison to this box of simple flowers. I put them in water and spent what seemed like hours just gazing at them. I was so excited that I even called my mother to gush. I even got a bit teary sitting there staring at them.

Flowers aren't expensive, nor are they particularity hard to send but their impression lingers. They make a woman feel like she is being courted. And since we are on the subject of old school courting—never underestimate the value of opening a few doors for her, opening the car door, or offering your jacket if she is cold. It doesn't matter if the two of you are more role-playing lesbians and you are usually the more femme one. Even a woman who fancies herself more butch can enjoy being treated to a bit of old fashioned chivalry every now and again. It's not necessarily masculine to open a door or pull out a chair. It may seem more like a man's action, but really it just shows respect and care.

Today I want you to simply send your woman a bouquet. If she's a stay at home mom, send them to the house (but make sure you aren't home when they arrive). If she is a career gal, send them to her office. Try to find flowers that mean something—they needn't be roses. However, some might say that roses are the most romantic flower to get. Perhaps she has a favorite flower? Perhaps you want to send her a flower that if she were to Google the flowers' significance, it will reveal its meaning. For example, lilies mean faith. Red signify romance, orange means passion, etc. It doesn't matter what kind of flower you send, just the act of sending them, along with a lovely and thoughtful note is what is important.

Now for the note. As we know, from an earlier chapter, sending notes is easy. The note you attach to the arrangement should be similar but not the same as the ones you have hidden away in her wallet. I can't tell you exactly what to write because it should come from the heart, but the note is ultimately more important than the flowers. If you have a nickname for your woman, of course, use that to address her. Your note can say that you miss her, that you will be waiting with bated breath for her to get home to you tonight or whatever you think will make her smile. If she has a special nickname for you, sign off with that.

Now once you have chosen the perfect bouquet and written a romantic note, don't stop there. Buy a single rose and lay it on her pillow. Attach another small note to that. Small gestures mean so much. They make a woman feel cherished and treasured. Personally, I would rather a woman send me a rose that she hopes will make me swoon than just calling the local jeweler to send me an expensive bracelet. I realize I may be in the minority here, but expensive gifts never moved me as much as those from the heart. Call me a hopeless romantic but I believe that it's the small thoughtful things that leave the most lasting impressions. For example, one of my exes gave me six almost identical teddy bears for Christmas. We spent a lot of time naming them. We agonized for months after that, trying to tell them apart with the names we had given them. When my friends asked what I got for Christmas and I told them, some gave me a look that said, "That's all?" But for me, that gift meant so much and even now, long after that relationship ended, I still look at those bears and smile.

You can never buy someone's love, so it's silly to even try. I know many women whose attention can be bought with expensive gifts, but not their love—women like that are best to stay clear of. Those are the women who go after power lesbians with money, marry them and then walk away with half of their fortune. Beware. You should never feel a need to shower a woman with expensive gifts. If you want to buy her something that special do it because you want to, not because she expects it. The power in presenting your girlfriend with a thoughtful gift that was picked out especially for her will go a long way. She will feel like one in a million! At the end of the day, that is all that anybody really wants from her partner.

Simone Reyes

Chapter Sixteen

Day 13- Cool Girlfriends Go Commando

Ladies, ladies, ladies, if I may toot my own horn here for just one moment please allow me this opportunity. I may not know cars, finance or sports (the list goes on and on) but lingerie I know. I know lingerie the way Carrie Bradshaw knows shoes, the way, Dolly Parton knows wigs, the way Kim Kardashian knows her best side for a selfie, the way Martina Navratilova knows tennis, the way Ellen DeGeneres knows sneakers, the way Dita Von Teese knows burlesque, the way Courtney Cox knows Botox… you know what I am saying. I know everything there is to know about pretty, sexy, hot underwear. I have enough of the stuff to open a brothel. It literally takes up all of my drawer space. I love pretty, frilly, naughty, and sexy under things. I don't just wear it for my partner either. I like knowing that under my jeans, business suit, sweat pants or whatever I am wearing, that I have on something beautiful. I especially love to rock boy's underwear (more on that later.) So if you haven't guessed, I am sending you shopping!

Now, for the tomboy types, I don't want to lose you here, stay with me for a moment while I cater to the more girlie girls first. Girls, if you have a store called Agent Provocateur in your town head there first. In my opinion, they are the leaders of the totally awesome under things pack. The first sign that tells me I'm really into a girl is when my feet steer me to Agent Provocateur. I should warn you, AP will cause a deep dent in your wallet, but it really is a treat for your girlfriend and for yourself. If there isn't one in your town, look at their website. If that shop doesn't do it for you I will bet anything you have a mall that has a Victoria's Secret for you to drop some cash in. So, for you femme girls let's get you lookin' really naughty! I want you to go and purchase some really over-the-top stuff. If your local lingerie place isn't quite naughty enough, log on to the Frederick's of Hollywood site. They have it all! I want you to buy garter belts, push up bras, crotchless panties, thigh high stockings (the ones with the seam in the back are my personal fave) and a sheer, see-through nightgown. Spend as much cash as you feel comfortable spending but do try to buy at least one of the things I mentioned.

Simone Reyes

Thank you for your patience, my more tomboy types. I know that some of us would never be caught dead in anything frilly or crotch-less. No prob. If it turns you on to wear leather (as a vegan, I would prefer you don pleather—no animal needs to die for fashion!) chaps, nipple clamps, bondage vests, etc. go ahead and rock it. If you prefer briefs or boxers, go for it! American Apparel makes a variety of men's cut styles that are made to flatter a women's shape and you can get a matching wife beater. It sizzles! Or go out and purchase a pair of men's underwear at the men's store that you absolutely love. Just be sure that it flatters your body and expresses your personal style.

Now make a date with your woman for dinner tonight. If finances are an issue, you can take her to your local diner. If you can splurge a little, make a reservation at a dark, candlelit spot. Put on your new treasure under your clothes, with your woman none the wiser. On the way to the restaurant tell her you are wearing something special for her but you "forgot" to show it to her back at home. She will be intrigued so flash her a peek of your new purchase.

Go to dinner and order your entrée. Then before it comes, tell her to sit tight as you go to the ladies room.

In the ladies room, I want you to remove one piece of underwear. It should be either your bra or your briefs/panty. Return to the table and hand it to her under the table. Tell her you want to see what she will look like in it later. How nice of you to share! A casual, routine meal will never be boring when underwear is exchanged under the table. Keep the conversation light and flirtatious. Remind her you are naked under your pants, skirt or shirt. Sex will be on the brain now so don't be surprised if you never make it to dessert. Hell, you may not make it through dinner at all. But try to; you will require more than a bit of fuel for later—just don't overdo it. Dessert will be waiting for you at home. And she will be wearing your underwear when it is served.

The rest of your ensemble I want you to wear on another evening. Get a trench coat and put on a corset, garters, stockings and heels. Meet your woman at her office or at a dinner you have scheduled ahead of time. When nobody is looking pull her aside and open your coat. Tell her you were feeling naughty today thinking about her and wanted to play. When you get home, this may lead to sex. It may not. But no matter what it should make her smile. If you would never be caught dead in a corset, feel free to wear something else that makes you feel sexy under your coat.

Chapter Seventeen

Day 14- Cool Girlfriends Take Their Girlfriend on Cool Adventures

What adventure have you and your partner discussed doing that you just never got around to planning? Hand gliding? Parasailing? Whitewater Rafting? Salsa Lessons? Surfing? For you couch potatoes—an apple picking trip? A pumpkin patch hunt? Movies in a park? Disneyland? Or for you "don't like to move much for any reason" types—an art gallery opening? Knitting class? A parade (Pride of course!)? Kite flying? Whale watching? Basically, the options are endless. Go on the Internet and find an adventure suited to both of you and make time to do it as soon as possible. Today if you can. Make the plans together as it will increase the excitement to go through all of the details as a unit. If you decide to do something really adventurous, it will pay off better than something more boring. Often when two people go through something new and exciting together, it creates an immediate bonding experience.

The trip will forever be a place you can happily revisit in conversation and will provide a lasting memory.

It's important to take both physical and mental snapshots of the times when you are really happy, connected and feeling great about your relationship. If you like to be on social media, take pics of your adventure and post them. Two women in love will want to show the world how happy they are. If your girlfriend or wife doesn't show you off, then you are probably with the wrong person. Or vice versa. You can tell a lot about a relationship by how proud your partner is to have you on their arm. Start to document all of the happy times the two of you share. These photos will show your growth (or should I say regrowth) as a couple and can do wonders to help steady a shaky relationship. That said, be in the moment. Please do not become a slave to your device.

It's sad, pathetic and enraging to have to include this, but even in this day and age, walking down the street in broad daylight with your gay lover can be unnerving. I'm from Greenwich Village in New York City—basically the capitol of "out" and just the other day I was shocked to hear some ignorant idiot shouting insults at two men holding hands in front of me. If you live in Middle America, I understand how public displays of affection can still make some of you anxious or uncomfortable. That said, whenever it's possible to take a snapshot of a happy moment, I say go for it. Photographs of you both as a couple—happy, smiling, hugging and kissing- are something you should have on record for the entire world to see. The days of being in the closet should be behind every LGBT person and if we continue to hide, we will never truly be free.

Make sure when you are on your exciting adventure, whatever it is, that you make it a point to whisper in her ear, touch her and love her. Be present in that moment. There is nothing like the power of NOW.

Chapter Eighteen

Day 15- Cool Girlfriends Know How To Serve Dinner Right

If you haven't treated yourself to the movie classic *Nine and a Half Weeks*, please do so immediately. First of all, you will probably dream of Kim Bassinger for a few nights—she is that breathtaking in this role (just don't share that with your girlfriend!) Pop in the movie and pause it at the food scene. For those of you who have yet to see it, in one hot scene Kim and Mickey Rourke (pre-plastic surgery) are lit only by the light from a refrigerator. They take turns using blindfolds as they hand feed each other a variety of foods. Some of the foods are bitter, some sweet. Some burn their mouth, some comfort with a chill. In no time, it becomes a sexually charged game and there is food that is gooey, silky, crunchy, slippery—you name it—dripping all over Kim, up her legs and down her shirt. They look like they are having a ball and it is very erotic.

Simone Reyes

Food is one of the most fun things to incorporate into lovemaking. Go to the store with this in mind and purchase a bunch of finger foods, various types and tastes, two blindfolds and a shower curtain liner. Try exotic new foods that you both are unfamiliar with. Of course, go and get some whipped cream. I am a vegan but cannot imagine not having whipped cream. Lucky for me, there is a vegan one! Try to get home before your girl and set out a picnic on your bed with all the foods laid out on a picnic blanket. Make sure you lay a shower curtain liner over the sheets on your bed. Those expensive sheets must not get ruined later on!

When she gets home have her join you. Tell your girlfriend you will be in charge of feeding her tonight. Tell her it's going to be a new adventure for her mouth. Then ask if you may blindfold her. Tell her to trust you- that this is going to be a lot of fun. Make sure she isn't wearing an expensive couture outfit. If she is, have her change into something that can get messy.

Have a variety of foods available. Again I am vegan, so these are my suggestions: cold pasta, hot red peppers, cake, limes, lemons, rice dream ice cream, vegan whipped cream, chocolate sauce, ice, fruit, soymilk, chocolate almond milk, water, etc. Remember, these are appetizer type of foods, the real dinner you can have later. Once she is blindfolded, have her open her mouth and stick out her tongue. Put a piece of pasta on it, follow it with something hot, like the pepper. When her mouth burns a bit, follow with the cold soymilk… you get the idea. Then, once you have allowed her to have a taste of everything take an ice cube. Run it over her lips, her mouth, allow it to find her neck, her collarbone, her décolleté. Then, have the ice cube find her breast, her nipple and move it around in a circular motion so it gets her nipple erect. Open her blouse and continue to play with the ice cube on her nipple. Lick the water off. Really spend some time worshipping her breasts, allowing the interplay between the cold ice and your warm mouth to arouse her. Drip chocolate sauce on her. Lick it off. Squeeze an orange over her body. Keep it sensual. Once you get her worked up move the party to the bedroom. Once there, take off her blindfold and kiss her.

Again, only advance if she seems receptive. If she does, take the chocolate sauce and vegan whipped cream (and any other goodies you want to play with) and let them all drip over her body. Hopefully you have already laid out the shower curtain over your bed linens so that the mess is contained. Use the whipped cream and spray some on her breasts and on her pussy. Take your time licking it off. Try some finger painting with the chocolate sauce; make a mess using your hands, lips, tongue and mouth to eat off her body.

Switch places and have her do the same to you. Enjoy the playfulness with each other and then finish off with a shared, relaxing bath.

Chapter Nineteen

Day 16- Cool Girlfriends Speak Erotically; Tell Her Somethin' Good

Now that you have learned how to walk the walk, it's time to talk the talk—the erotic talk that is. The power of a woman's voice can sound as smooth as a cat purring. Just the sound of a silky, low voice can get a girl dizzy, get her panties wet and make her come. Yes, come. The voice is a potent, important instrument that can unleash sexual passion.

First, before you even contemplate what you want to convey, lower your pitch, slow down your words and steady your breathing. You never want to speak erotically above a whisper. Erotic talk must invite your girlfriend to lean in a bit to hear all the wonderful, sensual words that will be dripping from your mouth. To get things started, practice speaking erotically when you are alone. If you aren't completely comfortable verbalizing words such as clit, pussy, poonany, yoni, muff, etc. start now. If you and your girl haven't engaged in explicit sex talk before, let's not rush into unknown territory.

Pay a visit to your local bookstore and browse their lesbian erotica section. Choose a book that you will feel comfortable reading to your woman. Fortunately, your local bookstore should carry a few good selections or if not, there's always Amazon.

When you get home and are tucked away in bed with her take it out. Read it to yourself and then ask if you can read to her a bit. Keep your voice low and sultry. This is perfect practice for the time when you will be speaking erotically to her off your own script.

The next time you are in bed giving her a massage or sharing a bath, get close to her ear. Start to touch her in a sexual way and whisper in her ear something like, "I am getting so wet just looking at you" or "you have the most beautiful pussy I have ever seen"…you get the vibe. If you get the impression that you can be more bold, you can add in something like, "I want to lick your clit right now" or "I'm going to fuck you all night baby" You know your lover and her taste, so just go with what you are feeling. If she seems uncomfortable, soften it up a bit. During sex, women really enjoy a bit of a cheering section. If she is doing something that you are enjoying—tell her. As Madonna says, "Express Yourself!"

However, you should never feel you need to fake it! Don't put on a verbal show. In hetero porn or even in movies, it is common for a man to barely touch a woman before she tosses her head back and begins to moan in ecstasy. My apologies to any males who may be reading this (although I'd be surprised to hear if any of 'em are) but many women tend to fake pleasure, or at least exaggerate it if they aren't in the mood.

The next time you find yourself in an intimate moment with your girl, begin to verbalize what you are seeing and feeling. There may be nothing sexier than a woman whispering in her woman's ear while they are making love. You can get perfect access to her ear when you are on a top/bottom position, rubbing each other, doin' the hump or fingering each other.

Another good position for erotic talk is with your girl's back to you, hand wrapped around her hip entering her pussy with your fingers from the front. Some positions are just not the best choices for erotic talk—those would be 69 (it may be easier to send a telegram) or oral sex. It's nice to lift up your head and say something like "you taste so good" but anything more than that is a distraction for the both of you.

Erotic talk is a great tool to use when you are away from each other. Call her when you know she isn't in a meeting or busy with the kids and begin your erotic talk as soon as she answers the phone. Don't allow the conversation to head into familiar territory such as what to pick up at the grocery store on the way home. It should go something like this.

> Ring: Hello?
> You: Hey, babe I was just thinking about you.
> Her: Yeah? What were you thinking?
> You: I was thinking about your pussy.
> Her: (Surprised) Really?
> You: I was thinking that of all the women in (insert your home state here) I am the luckiest one because my girl has the sweetest tasting pussy—like a delicious, sweet peach. I just want to slide my fingers up inside you tonight and drive you wild.

If she seems receptive, you can see if she feels loose enough to try it herself. Try to open the door for her by starting off this part of the conversation with something like…

You: What do you feel when I tell you that? Tell me what you like and I will do it tonight when you get home…

Either she will tell you all about it or she won't but at least you have opened up a safe space for her to consider it.

If this goes as well as I anticipate, at this point you may hear the phone drop, she may jump in her car and head home or if she can't get away, your words will hang in the air beckoning her. Keep up with it!

Whenever you have a sexual thought about your woman or her body, make it known. Verbalize it. Don't worry you won't seem like a perv! She wants to know how you feel when you see her naked body—every woman does. Switch it up, sometimes make the talk about how you feel about her spirit, her soul and other times just talk dirty. Speak your truth softly and it will be music to her ears. Send her text messages that say short and to the point messages like "You should be naked in our bed" or "I want to taste you right now." Soon she will be checking her phone every minute hoping for another word from you.

Chapter Twenty

Day 17-Cool Girlfriends Watch Porn

It's certainly no secret that die-hard feminist lesbians will probably not be so keen to support the porn industry in any way. All I can say to that is I respect your decision. However, there are adult entertainment companies that not only cater to lesbians but also are run by them. Perhaps that bit of info may help you make a decision to watch or not. Porn can be a fun, harmless and instrumental tool to help get things movin' when the sea is calm. For those of you who are willing to welcome porn into your sex life you must first ask yourself a few questions before you order that flick: is your girlfriend a breast girl, an ass girl? Is she bisexual and likes to watch two straight people get it on? Do her tastes run more extreme? Does she enjoy watching gangbangs? Maybe some S&M? Spanking? Gay men's porn? Does she have a fetish? If you don't know the answers to these questions, you better find out because it's movie night!

Simone Reyes

All women are different. Some women are immediately turned off by soft and hard-core porn. If you or your girlfriend is in this category, I recommend starting slowly with a mainstream movie that has some girl–girl action. My favorites are *Loving Annabelle, Desert Hearts, Bound, Blue Is The Warmest Color* and for fans of the classics, *Personal Best*. If you both start off with these, you can graduate to more hardcore art. When used correctly, porn is like the cliff notes to a big sex test—it is so helpful, it seems illegal. Watching other people have sex can be a huge turn on. However, it should only be used in moderation or it can become a crutch. Think of it like this: remember when you were learning to swim as a kid and the instructor put those arm floaters on you? How easy it would have been to float around, hardly doing any work and never really learning how to swim on your own. Easy yes, but ultimately a mistake. Porn will most likely get the two of you aroused and chances are a good porn movie will make you want to get it on. Just remember, use it sparingly. Your woman's body is a playground—if you really view it as such, you can decide to order up a porn flick, but you will never need it.

When you tell your girl you want to check out some porn, start by just sitting close to her. The night doesn't require ending with a sexual encounter, but of course that is the goal. As you feel yourself heating up, glance at your woman. See if you can tell that she seems to be getting turned on. Put your hand on her thigh and ask if she is getting wet. Chances are if the porn is a good one she will be. Tell her how much hotter she is than the girl on screen; how much you prefer her smaller or larger breasts. If she seems receptive, put your arm around her and pull her closer. If you are on a couch or in bed, snuggle in closer. Touch yourself if the moment feels right. Take her hand and put it on your genitals. Turn her head to you and kiss her neck and then her lips. Don't be surprised if this goes all the way tonight. If for whatever reason it doesn't remember this is a process. And it's only Day 17—that dragon may still have some strength left. Be patient and stay open to the possibilities of what is next.

Chapter Twenty-One

Day 18-Cool Girlfriends Like to Watch and Be Watched

I am going to tell it to you straight. This chapter may make some of you a tad uncomfortable—especially if you are prone to shyness. Don't worry, I am here to hold your hand and get you through this. Nobody, believe it or not, is shyer than myself. Nobody. And yet, when my woman needs to see me at my most erotic you can bet on me to deliver. Why? Because I care. You are going to need some supplies before we get started: an alarm clock (or just set your cell phone as an alarm), a vibrator (bet you already have one of those) and an open mind. We are going charge right into the world masturbation. If you and your girlfriend have never seen each other masturbate, you will now. Like I said, as someone who can be painfully shy when all that mushy love/sex stuff happens, I understand how it feels to be frozen with inhibition. However, here I am writing a book on those very topics so there is hope for us all. The best way to learn how to please a woman is to see how she pleases herself. If you think back to a time when you were actually having regular sex with your partner, you probably at the very least were told or shown how she likes to be touched.

However, at the time it was probably early in the relationship and chances are you were so concerned with learning and remembering it, it was probably more of a textbook lesson than an erotic display. Tonight it will be an erotic slideshow. Set your alarm for the middle of the night on a day when she doesn't have to get up very early the next day. If your vibrator isn't already in the bedside table drawer, put it there—and make sure it has fresh batteries! When your alarm goes off, awaken your girlfriend by kissing her gently on the neck. Do this for a while until she is awake but still in a semi-dream state. Put your hand in between her warm thighs and lightly touch her hips, her ass, and her thighs. Starting very slowly, gently and with a light touch begin to use your fingers to glide up and down her thighs. Make your way up and circle her pussy and eventually begin to touch her there. Continue doing this until she is aroused but not long enough to get her to the point of coming. Then take her hand and put it where yours is. I'm sure I don't have to remind you that as we get aroused we usually require consistent, steady movements. Therefore, you don't want to stop abruptly. Make sure she picks up the rhythm and the strength of pressure or she may lose the building sexual tension and it will take longer for her to climax. Tell her you want to watch her. Light a candle or put on a nightlight. Keep it dim.

Take out the vibrator and tell her it's nearby should she want to incorporate it but only if she gets into trouble finishing herself off. She may feel embarrassed, but whisper in her ear how hot she looks and how beautiful she is. While you are watching her you will certainly be getting very turned on. Feel free to touch yourself but if you feel you can't keep your eyes on your girl, try to control yourself. I want your eyes glued to her. If you feel that you can hold out until after she climaxes tell her to watch you bring yourself to orgasm. The point of this exercise is to create a bonding experience. It takes a lot of trust for women to climax in front of anyone, even when they are madly in love, it can be very tough on a shy girl- let alone when they are the only one in charge of their orgasm and all the attention is on them. Once this is shared, whether this is the first time or you have seen her masturbate many times in your relationship, it's an important moment to enjoy and helps rebuild intimacy. After the two of you have finished, hold her close until she drifts back off to sleep. The next morning over coffee, whisper in her ear, how hot it was to watch her touch herself that way. And thank her for that special gift.

Chapter Twenty-Two

Day 19- Cool Girlfriends Have Got a Pole, Will Strip (and Give Lap Dances!)

The ancient art of the strip tease has been a part of the world's culture since nearly the beginning of time. Assuming you are a lesbian, I don't have to tell you that the woman's body is the most beautiful form on earth. Seeing it slowly, methodically, painstakingly unveiled one garment at a time can be downright hypnotizing.

Later in this chapter in the "Cool Girlfriends Give Lap Dances," section I address any issues you may have—political or otherwise—that may cause you to question if stripping or lap dancing is really for you. Feel free to jump ahead and read the beginning of it so that you can feel secure. I put those responses in the lap dance section because while stripping and lap dances usually go hand in hand, lap dances are ultimately more difficult to do if a woman has reservations about it—emotionally and even, physically.

Slaying the Lesbian Bed Death Dragon

Let me begin by easing your mind; not all strippers need to look like Pamela Anderson. In fact, every woman—femme, butch, overweight, out of shape, etc. can perform a sensuous, sexy strip for her girlfriend that will, with my help, outshine any strip she has ever seen. Even my stone butches: you take your clothes off at night right? Well, for this exercise it's the same thing but you will be taking them off to music—very, very slowly. I understand that this will be more of a challenge for some of you depending on your comfort zones but stay the course.

When your girl gets home say simply, "I want to show you something." You don't have to explain any more than that. Put her on the couch or in a chair. Turn on some sexy music, turn off the lights and set the stage.

Let's begin with my girls who like to dress up: you will have the full strippers ensemble—a short, sexy outfit that will be peeled away to reveal a G-string and lace bra, or nothing, depending on how you feel once you get into the groove. For all of you who do not like typically feminine clothing, you will be stripping off a buttoned up shirt or something on the tomboy side, down to a pair of boxers or briefs and a wife beater tank. Fun, fun… FUN!

For me, this chapter is one of the most awesome chapters in the book. I can't wait to teach you how to amaze and excite your girlfriend, while empowering yourself, so let's get right to it!

Stripping is about teasing, withholding, suspense, eye contact, flirting and ultimately a big, fat NO holds barred extraordinary reward. When you are doing a strip you are presenting yourself to your lover and yet keeping yourself like a secret just beyond her reach.

The outfit should represent you, but take it up a notch. You can strip out of a men's suit, a dress, and a pair of jeans, basically anything that doesn't take a million years to undo. Strippers never struggle with laces or zippers. Movements must be slow and fluid.

For my second group, my ladies who fancy themselves to be more androgynous or butch, put together an outfit that consists of a pair of boxers/ briefs, a wife beater, tie, a men's shirt and you will be all set (and feel free to strap on your dildo if you desire).

Group one: put on a push up bra, a pair of tiny stripper shorts, a G-string, mini skirt, tank top, cardigan and a pair of six-inch stilettos. If you want to throw in a masculine edge, put on a baseball cap backwards and switch out the heels for Converse sneakers. Delish! Both outfits seem quite different but they each involve layers and this is all that is necessary for a strip. Each garment will be peeled away… so delicious, so luscious, and so good.

    Begin by making the room look enticing. Make sure you have the lights turned down low with the main light in the room positioned behind you. Drape it with a scarf for extra affect. Choose a sexy song that you love. Some great songs to strip to are Beyonce's "Drunk In Love," Joe Cocker's "You Can Leave Your Hat On," Prince's "Sexy Mother F**ker," Lorde's " Royals" and my all time favorite, David Banner's "Play". No country music please. I love country music and listen to it all the time but it is not typically strip tease worthy, so skip those songs completely. Other than that rule, use whatever song gets you hot. Sit your girlfriend down on a couch/chair, as far away from you as you can—you may need to clear out some furniture to give you a bit of free space. Tell her a show is about to begin and that she has a front row seat.

Simone Reyes

When you feel ready to begin, put on the music and let yourself sway and get into the song before you start moving. Allow yourself to get out of your head, think about the lyrics, feel the bass, and lose yourself in the movement.

Remember this tip: Do not make eye contact with your lover until you are removing a piece of clothing. This eye contact will be like a silent communication; your eyes will be asking if she wants to see more of you—and babe, she will. Then once you remove a piece of clothing you will look away so that her eyes can savor every inch of your body.

Now that the music has started and you feel it enter your body, begin to sway. For my butch gals, you don't have to exaggerate your hip movements. I hate to reference Chippendale dancers for a million and one obvious reasons, but they don't move like female strippers, and yet they do move. They dance but their movements exaggerate more muscles—flexing and such. Try to think of that if you are in no way going to use any feminine dance steps here. You can also strut around, playing with your tie and flipping your hat. Just have fun, but try to keep your movements slow. We lose our power when we move quickly.

Group 2, make small circles with your hips and put your hands in your hair. Exaggerate your hips, make your movements big and round. If you are wearing a hat, let your fingers follow the brim and tip. Always keep both hands moving over your body. Allow your hands to touch your body the way you want your lover to caress you. It looks really great when your hands are moving in opposite directions. For example, one hand is heading north to your collarbone, massaging your neck while your other hand is reaching down south circling your crotch.

While you are standing in front of your woman, allow your hips to continue making small circles as you begin to undo your top. If you are packing, touch your "cock" and make her want it.

Whether you will be peeling off a men's shirt or a cardigan, both should be buttoned up, but only three buttons. Undo one-button and lock eyes with your woman. Your eyes will be asking her, "Should I undo this button?" The mental message will of course be yes so undo one for her. Undo it slowly and seductively. Then take your eyes off of her and walk around, still swaying to the music. If you are wearing a tie, loosen it now and pull it slowly over your head. Toss it in her direction. Fall down (gracefully) on your knees and continue with your hip circles. Or for my more butch gals, try a bit of hip thrusting: keep the movements more back to front rather than round and big.

Let your hands find your hair and play with it or have them fall over your hips, loving your curves. If your hair is short use a slicking back motion, similar to the way James Dean worked his fingers through his hair. If you are wearing a hat, play with it, tucking it down to hide your eyes and then eventually taking it off and tossing it.

Slowly undo a button from your jeans/pants or mini skirt. Pull the garment slowly down past your hips and then down past your ass. Lower yourself onto your butt so that you are sitting on the floor. Drop your knees to the side. Lower yourself onto your back, using your arms and elbows to brace you. Once on your back begin prancing (this looks like a slow bicycle move like you do in gym class) with your legs. Try arching your back for effect. This will look amazing. Once your legs are in the air out in front of you doing a slow bicycle move, begin to slowly move the garment down and over past your thighs, knees, calf and ankles. Then kick it off. Once the mini skirt or jeans/pants are off, roll onto your stomach slowly. Your girlfriend now has a great shot of your ass—covered in a brief or a pair of stripper shorts.

From the on your back position, slowly rise up. Your rise up should be painfully slow. Try to keep your head and chest down on the floor and rise up as slowly as you can. Drag yourself up to a sitting position. Gracefully, get back onto your knees. Glance at her again and begin to undo a few more buttons on your shirt or cardigan. Again, glance at your lover asking if she wants to see more. Before you undo the last button slowly, painstakingly rise. Turn around with your back to her. Undo the last button and look over your shoulder as you let the shirt fall down to the floor.

At this point, your butt should be covered by boxers /briefs (maybe you are packing), or you are down to wearing only a pair of small stripper shorts. Either way, stand and face a wall. Walk slowly over to the wall and position yourself as if you are being arrested- legs spread apart, hands on the wall, head low. It should look like a police officer is frisking you. Sway your butt back and forth, allowing her to get a good look at your luscious backside. Then stand up straight and turn around. Now, if you are wearing a wife beater and no bra, turn back around and face your lover, still swaying to the music. Tug on the bottom of your shirt, pulling it down and lifting it up in a teasing way. Now turn your back to her but tilt your head around to look at her over your shoulder. With your arms criss-crossed across your chest, with your eyes locked with your woman's, slowly begin to lift the tank over your stomach, breasts, neck and finally (but slowly) pop it over your head. For those of you who are wearing a bra we are going to do the same move as above with the wife beater but when you are facing away from her, unhook your bra slowly. Then, turn just your head around, keeping your back to her. Maintain eye contact with her; your eyes telling her that the bra will be coming off but not a moment too soon. Once you unhook the bra, allow one strap to fall over your shoulder, then the other and with one final glance, allow the bra to fall to the floor. Now the wife beater and the bra are both on the floor. It's the moment she has been waiting for-turn around and let your woman finally see your beautiful breasts. What happens next is up to the two of you. If you want to continue over to her, you can slowly peel down to your G-string or if you are packing you can peel your briefs down to reveal your strap on. It's your paradise island, baby—do what comes naturally.

Now for you serious strippers, I want to encourage any woman who wants to tune in fully to her erotic side to enroll in stripper class. Many cities have pole classes – the best one in my opinion is Sheila Kelley's S Factor. Luckily for women everywhere Sheila is opening up new studios across the globe every day it seems. In these classes you will learn the moves of professional strippers and more importantly, you will learn to love your body and empower yourself. Not only will you learn to strip like a pro and give lap dances like a real stripper but you will learn how to fly on a pole.

Women everywhere are not only taking these classes but are having poles installed in their homes. If you decide to take such a class your lover will be instantly graduated to being the coolest lesbian on the block – hands down. Listen, any woman who is lucky enough to have her girl do pole tricks for her- is lucky enough! End of story.

Part 2: Cool Girlfriends Give Lap Dances

First of all, I think it may be safe to assume one of two things: One, as a lesbian you have either visited a strip club or paid for a lap dance or you have fantasized about getting one. But, have you actually given one? If the answer is no, don't fret. You will soon. You are going to love the power a lap dance gives you. Your girlfriend is going to love it as well because a lap dance is a treat that not every woman can say she gets to enjoy in the privacy of her own home. She may have trouble recognizing you as you transform yourself into someone that can confidently pull off one of the sexiest moves under the sun. I know, you are probably having many doubts, so let's get those out of the way pronto!

Doubt # 1- "I'm a feminist, how can I condone stripping?"

The short answer is: this is going to be in the privacy of your own home, for your own lover. There are no men throwing dollar bills at you—it's all in fun. The longer answer has no place here; it's a political and personal debate. Personally, I support the choice of any woman to hold whatever job she desires. So, long story short, don't overthink this. At the end of this chapter, you are going to know how to turn your lover's switch back to the "on" position. 'Nuff said.

Doubt #2- "I'm too butch."

In *Flashdance*, Jennifer Beals looked pretty butch behind her mask in her welding outfit too but at night she was strutting her stuff in a red teddy on a stage like nobody's business. Ok, so you don't look like Jennifer Beals and you feel uncomfortable taking on a "girly" type of role. No problem. There are many variations giving a lap dance. Maybe you will just never feel comfortable wearing anything "girlier" than men's underwear or boy shorts and a wife beater tank- so what? You can still give a killer lap dance that will have your girlfriend begging for more, even if you will never wear something that looks very revealing. In fact, it's worth mentioning that personally I have never in my life seen any woman look sexier than when she is wearing a nothing but a pair of Hugo Boss/Calvin Klein underwear. Cool girlfriends can rock any outfit so long as she feels sexy and desirable in it.

Doubt #3- "I'm too old/fat/out of shape/have to much cellulite," and other self-sabotaging thoughts.

Remember, nobody has the perfect body. We all have things we wish were different when we look in the mirror. There is no reason to feel insecure being "on display" in front of your lover. Do you really think that movie stars look flawless without the right lighting, body make up and airbrushing? They don't. Trust me, I have worked in the entertainment field for years, so I know this first hand. Having experience in front of the camera and behind it, I have been mesmerized by the tricks that are used to make people look perfect on film and in magazines. In this chapter, I will help you to not only to look your best, using some of the oldest stripper secrets in the book, but will also help you understand that its not so much how you look but how you work how you look. Honey don't be concerned, I've got you covered.

Doubt #4- "My girlfriend is going to laugh at me and I'm going to look like a fool."

Babe, I've got news for you: your girlfriend would much rather have a fire burning out of control down below than to hose it down with a belly laugh. The key is if you believe you are sexy then your girlfriend will believe it too. If you make it a joke then she will see it as a joke as well. It's that simple. However, don't get me wrong, a bit of giggling is completely appropriate when giving a show if that's what you are feeling. It's not about making her laugh though; it's about making her hot. And hotness is going to be on the agenda for the night and for many nights to come! You are going to look like a superstar and the stage is going to be set for seduction.

Candles are going to be creating the perfect mood lighting. A correctly positioned lamp is going to back light you. Your girlfriend is going to have her eyes completely glued to you. She will be deeply intrigued by what you have planned for her. Then she will be excited by it, even flattered that you have gone this far to impress her. Finally, she will be catapulted back to the first time she got (or dreamed of getting) a lap dance. She will remember the feeling of sitting on her hands in a Champagne Room in a strip club somewhere and wanting to reach out and touch that gorgeous woman who was doing hip circles on her lap. However, this time, lucky for her, the girl who will be driving her wild will be someone she knows very well and someone who she just may get lucky with. IF she gets lucky, that is. Like Justin Timberlake says, we are "bringing sexy back."

Now that we have gotten those nasty and silly thoughts out of the way, let's get down to learning how to give a killer lap dance. It is not necessary to do the strip and the lap dance on the same night. You can either do them together or on separate days- see how it goes.

Personally, I prefer to do them together with the lap dance smack in the middle of a strip but you may want to save up the lap dance for another night. Or your girlfriend just may beg you for one—it will be your choice. It's your world!

Things you will need: a sexy outfit of your choice- layered so that you can slip out of more than one thing, a playlist (with speakers) and dim lighting. For that, consider purchasing an amber or red light bulb, a scarf to drape over a lamp or using candles. Perfume or cologne will heighten the mood. Finish off with a little lip gloss. Don't forget of course a comfy chair/couch that can hold the weight of both you and your girlfriend.

When you decide tonight is the night you are going to give your girlfriend a lap dance, make sure the phone is turned off so that you won't have any interruptions. Make sure she has eaten dinner and that she isn't too tired.

Whisper in her ear that you think she looks amazing tonight and that she deserves a treat. Disappear into the bedroom or bathroom and change into something you love, something that unleashes the erotic creature in your soul and gives you a feeling of self-confidence. For those of you with long hair, make sure it's free flowing.

Turn off the television; dim the lights, light a candle or two. Make sure whatever dim light is going to be on is positioned behind you (drape a scarf over it to dim it farther).

As I touched on earlier, positioning a light behind you gives a breathtaking outline of your body. It is also a way to hide imperfections. The backlight effect will create a beautiful silhouette and make your flaws seem to disappear. She will see the curves of your body as you move, which is mesmerizing. Don't forget your favorite cologne—doesn't matter if its aftershave or perfume—just make sure you smell delicious.

Then, put on your favorite lap dance song. This is going to be entirely a personal choice that I can't help you with but I will give you a word of caution. Recently, I was at my stripping class in New York City when the instructor put on a song by Lucinda Williams called "Those Three Days." The words seemed to be written just for me and sent me right back to experience the pain of a particular relationship in my past all over again. Before I knew what was happening, I was crying my eyes out—in stripper class! What a mess. So, make sure you choose a song that is positive and uplifting. Remember in *A League of Their Own* the famous line, "There's no crying in baseball!" Well, there's no crying in stripping either! Choose your song carefully. Slow songs tend to work better than fast ones but again, it's entirely your call. Your relationship by now is on the way back to Blissville, so be sure to choose a song that reflects hope and love and yes, sex. When in doubt, Prince is always a great choice.

Once you have the scene set, tell your lover to sit on a chair or couch. Make sure that it has an arm rest and isn't so small that it will tip over when you start to climb on it. Let the music start and close your eyes. Move your body to the song and melt like wax into the moment before you start towards your girl.

I think the sexiest way to start a lap dance is to crawl like a cat on the ground toward her. If there is no way you would do this, just strut toward her s-l-o-w-l-y. The world should be moving like a dance in slow motion. Throw back your hair if you feel like it; it's a sexy move, employed by all strippers. Or just run your fingers through your hair off your face. The way to crawl like a stripper is to think of yourself like a cat. Get down onto your hands and knees in a basic crawl position. Your opposite legs and hands are going to be moving at the same time when you crawl. Exaggerate the movement as you start toward your girlfriend. Move slowly and slink across the floor. Keep your head heavy, hanging down low. This crawl is where your girl gets to see your back, the way your shoulders move. It's so lovely and seductive to watch this move. Remember to flip up your head quickly—it will send your hair flying. It will look amazing!

When you get to her, take both of her hands and place them in her lap, one hand on each thigh. Put your hands on the armrests and place your right knee between her legs on the chair or couch. Steady yourself by reaching over her shoulders and holding onto the back of the chair/couch. Pull yourself up onto the chair/couch, but don't rush. Move slowly. Breathe. Always remember to breathe.

Place your left knee on the armrest. This in itself is an oh-so-sexy move, therefore she will be getting very turned on already, I promise. Arch your back, still holding onto the chair and do chest circles in front of your girlfriend's face. You will feel this move in your back and in your hips. Your legs will be stationary -

positioned between her legs (right leg) and on the armrest (left leg). The girl in the stripper role can touch the one she is stripping for wherever she wants, the lucky girl getting the show cannot. Take a moment to whisper in her ear, "No touching". In the stripper role of course you are free to touch her face and her body but not in an overly familiar way. Real strippers are allowed to touch but remember they don't have intimate connections with the person in the chair. If your girl tries to touch you, gently hold her hands and place them at her sides. You are playing a fantasy role here so stick with the rules.

Now comes the moment where you will need to remember those rules because it's about to get sizzlin' hot. Lean in as if you are going to kiss your lover on the mouth. Allow your lips to almost touch and then suddenly move off to the side of her face and nuzzle her neck ever so lightly. Then switch sides and nuzzle the other side of her neck. Make sure to use your hair to tickle her face and neck but never make significant contact. Now is the moment to dismount for the first time. Take your left leg off the armrest and place it next to your right leg, so that both knees will momentarily be between her legs. At this point, your hands should still be holding onto the back of the chair/couch. Straighten your legs and allow your body to slide down hers onto the floor. This is the first time you should have some real contact with your girlfriend's body. Slide your pelvis, breasts and torso slowly down the length of her torso between her lovely legs. Stop briefly when you pass her crotch, take a good look, she will feel the heat from your stare—a small glimpse of what is to come later. At this point you are sure to see her getting hot, her hands will want to reach out to touch but this is not allowed. If she tries to touch you quickly and firmly place her hands back on her thighs. Be sure to keep your knees slightly bent as you reach the floor.

Now, just when your woman thinks she can't be tortured anymore, remove a piece of clothing. Preferably it will be your top. Get up and turn around and to show her your behind. Again, slow down, keep it well paced, there is no rush here. Arch your back and lower your butt so that it is hovering over her lap, never touching! Keep your feet on the floor (in between her legs and rock back and forth, moving your hips in small circles over her lap. Then when you hear her breath start to get deeper and faster you can drape your body over hers, with your legs slightly bent between her legs. This is my favorite part because it's intimate and yet there is no use of hands. Now, your head will be on her right shoulder and you can gaze lovingly into her eyes but don't linger long.

Simone Reyes

Slide down the length of her body making your way to the floor. Once you are on the floor in front of her slowly stand up and walk into the bedroom. Throw her a look that invites her to join you. I can virtually guarantee your woman will follow.

If she does, which I anticipate, then have a great night of lovemaking. If the LBD is still prevailing, don't worry; sometimes it takes quite a few strikes on the match to light the fire. We will get there; our game plan isn't over yet. If the dance doesn't end in lovemaking and you feel rejected or hurt, take a moment's pause. Go to your journal and write down how you are feeling. Get it all out and then return to your girlfriend. Keep it light; no pressure. What you don't want to do is to be aggressive. Sure you may be turned on, but take the cue from her. You can always have a moment with your vibrator later—right now this is about the two of you. There is nothing wrong with putting your hand on her leg and saying something sweet like, "It's ok to touch now." Maybe that is all she will need or maybe it's just not going to be tonight. If that is the case, be patient. Rome wasn't (re-)built in a day. We WILL get her lit; just be patient and if its not tonight, put the TV on and have a cuddle.

Slaying the Lesbian Bed Death Dragon

Additionally, you should feel pretty darn proud of yourself either way. It's a confident woman who can pull off a lap dance and a very fortunate girlfriend who is treated to one.

Simone Reyes
Chapter Twenty-Three

Day 20- Let The Games Begin

When was the last time you had game night at your house with just your girl? If you have kids, put them to bed. If you have companion animals walk them and give them their favorite toy. Put your phones on silent and settle in for a night of fun. Bust out the board games and make a sexy night of it.

This exercise can be done with any of your favorite board games—Monopoly, Scrabble or any other board game you enjoy. Simply make your own rules such as if you roll the dice and have to pay to pass " Go" you have to service your partner. Services can include, a foot/neck massage, a kiss, a flash of your breast.

Why not a game of Truth of Dare? Truth or Dare, as most of you Madonna fans know, is a game where one player allows the other to choose between answering a truthful question or take the dare. This game is a fantastic way to utilize your creative side. However, this is not the night to ask leading questions that are meant to entrap your lover. For example, this is not the night to ask if she still fantasizes about her ex-girlfriend or if she secretly stalks her Instagram and "likes" a post or two. The questions you should consider asking are more along the lines of "What is your favorite erogenous zone?" or "What is your naughtiest fantasy?" Once you have the answers to these questions feel free to use them on date nights in the future. Dares can be funny such as "I dare you right now to write a love sonnet to my pussy" or a bit terrifying such as streaking the neighborhood in the middle of the night (just don't get arrested!). The truth and dares are all up to you!

    As luck would have it, you can also order sexy board games online. Some that I have researched include Foreplay Dice (one dice says things like "touch," "massage," "lick," and others say "Above belly," "tush," etc.) Fortunately, there are several online LGBT gift shops that offer games such as Sex Card Games that include position cards and act out fantasy cards.

    The goal is not to win the game; the goal is to win the girl. Just because you share your home/mortgage/bank account with your partner, doesn't mean you get to be lazy. Bring fun back into the bedroom! Call out to your inner teenagers and give them a place to play! Getting to first, second and third base never gets old!

Chapter Twenty-Four

Day 21-Cool Girlfriends Give Gifts To Feed The Spirit

Today's assignment is to casually try to uncover a secret goal your girlfriend has always dreamed of accomplishing. If you are really lucky, you already know that she always wanted to be a certified scuba diver, learn to ride a motorcycle, drive stick, learn to fly a plane, write a children's book, etc. If not, you will need to drop some subtle hints. Or ask a mutual friend to suss out the situation for you. It shouldn't be that hard—we all have things we would love to try. Then get her a gift certificate or enroll her in a class to start her on her way.

Help your woman accomplish something that she has always wanted to do that will make her feel exhilarated, proud and alive. If you don't have enough money to purchase the flying lesson, then buy her a book on planes and tell her you will be saving up to get her that lesson. Give that gift when you can. A gift that shows her you know her deepest desires and want to help

Slaying the Lesbian Bed Death Dragon

her realize them is something she will treasure. Intimacy begins in the spirit—remember that.

Simone Reyes

Chapter Twenty-Five

Day 22 –Cool Girlfriends Give Back

Women are maternal. Some of the most loving moms I have ever met are lesbians or mothers to their companion animals. When you enter a lesbian home that has been blessed with children or a gaggle of rescue animals, the energy there is often so rich because the maternal vibes are literally bouncing off the walls in every direction. I have filled my life with my own babies—homeless dogs and cats. Being maternal is not only meant for human children. I find that a woman who truly loves her companion animal as much as she would love any baby she gave birth to is very sexy. Compassion is sexier any day than indifference.

It is also worth mentioning that this month has been very focused on the two of you. We agreed at the beginning of this book that was how it was going to be—and rightfully so. However, sometimes we need a break from ourselves. This is why today you should turn your attention outward.

Go on the Internet and find charitable situations where you can join your woman to volunteer. You will get the opportunity to see her maternal and sensitive side and believe me; this is a real turn on. There is nothing cooler, especially to a woman, than to see her lover's giving/selfless side. Perhaps the local pound needs a dog walker to give the shelter animals a ray of sunlight away from their dark cages once in awhile. Or perhaps the local children's hospital could use someone to come in dressed as a clown or needs a person to read to the kids as they get well. Perhaps a hospice needs a kind-hearted person to sit and hold the hand of a dying elderly patient who has no family. Have a yard sale and use the proceeds to buy something from a charities wish list and deliver it in person. Maybe your local LGBT youth group needs mentors to support them. The list of charities that would love some support is endless. Do try to find one that requires real personal interaction. While getting signatures for important petitions is important, save that kind of volunteering for another day. Really get yourselves involved in a way that will tug at your heartstrings.

I have found that women respond very strongly to seeing a maternal side emerge from their partner. If you both have children together you will already know what I mean. On the same hand, seeing ourselves helping the less fortunate is often a very healing thing we can do for our own soul. The more we like ourselves, the better partners we will be. Often seeing your girlfriend giving back in a self-less way can be one of the most powerful aphrodisiacs known to (wo)man. Try it. You will be grateful you did and so will the people/animals you are helping.

Then afterward tell her in detail how proud you are of her and of each other as a unit. Look her directly in the eye, seal it with a kiss. Enjoy it.

Chapter Twenty-Six

Day 23-Cool Girlfriends Conserve Water and Shower Together

Rub a dub dub ladies! The next time your woman takes a shower, why not surprise her by sliding in beside her? Once inside, wash her hair, her body, maybe shave her. Kissing and touching in a steamy shower is very, well, steamy. Try it. Or perhaps she prefers baths? Strip down and go in behind her. Let her head rest on your chest as you bathe her. Wash her back and gently massage her. The scalp is a heavenly place to be massaged.

Keep bubble bath on hand and bath fizzies. Make the bathtub into a luxurious experience. While there, why not pull down the shower massager and set it to the pulsate mode. You can use it make her come right there in the tub. Then switch positions and have her use it on you. If you don't have a shower attachment that reaches into the tub, you can always help position her clit directly under the faucet as you support her weight but its not nearly as comfortable.

Once you are both squeaky clean, dry and warm you may find that you just want to cuddle. This cozy moment may be a great time to engage in some tribadism. I actually cannot believe I am using that word because it seems a bit archaic. It's only natural when you are cuddling to start rubbing against each other, humping and grinding your pelvis on hers, so go for it. Many women can climax easily this way. Why not add that to the agenda tonight?

Then blanket her in comfort. Run a bath, wash her hair, give her a back rub in the tub. Why not treat your woman to this kind of pampering. It's much more caring than sexual and will make her feel loved. Wrap her in soft towels and gaze lovingly into her eyes. Make her feel safe and pampered tonight and the fireworks will be set off before you know it.

Chapter Twenty-Seven

Day 24- Cool Girlfriend's Book Hotel Sex

What is hotter than hotel sex? Uh, NOTHING! A big king sized bed, crisp white sheets, room service, pay per view, turn down service... hello! Book a room for the two of you—even a motel will do if your wallet is short on cash, but try for a really luxurious hotel if possible. Hotels can make you feel mysterious—like two people sneaking off for a clandestine affair. There are no dishes to clean, no laundry to sort; housecleaning comes with the bill—it's the perfect place to devote to lovemaking. You can take long baths, get a massage, jump up and down on the bed and just have fun. The night you spend at a hotel is your escape.

Of course, just like everything else in life it's best to plan ahead. First thing on the list should be to make sure you bring a red bulb and replace it with the white one the hotel will surely have. Bring some candles. Then call ahead to your local florist or have the concierge do it for you and order some lovely smelling arrangements for the room (make sure to scatter rose petals on the bed). Bring your own speakers if the hotel doesn't have an iPod dock/laptop with your favorite playlists cued up. Bring some champagne unless you are both sober. Make sure you can sleep in the next morning and of course, always have the "Do Not Disturb Sign" on the door.

Time spent at a hotel allows for precious moments to devote to your lover. Make a game of it! Make a no-clothing allowed in the room rule. The second you enter, make sure it's a "clothes off" zone. Order in a couples massage in the room. Then when the masseuse has left, tell your girl to stay put. Continue the massage yourself but hit all the places the masseuse didn't touch. Kneed and play with the skin around her vagina. Inch closer to her pussy and slide your fingers inside her, rhythmically getting her to climax. Continue the massage after she has had her orgasm. This lady will be absolutely blissful. She may even return the favor. The next morning order breakfast in bed and do it all over again. An orgasm first thing in the morning is the perfect way to greet a new day.

Many times, a night spent in a hotel—away from the mundane—is a great shot in the arm for a relationship that needs a boost. I will wager a bet that the

Slaying the Lesbian Bed Death Dragon

lesbian bed death dragon can't find its way to a hotel so it's a great hideaway until that dragon leaves town for good.

Chapter Twenty-Eight

Day 25 - Cool Girlfriends Make Videos

Today you will meet the voyeur in you. You will play both director and star and make a sex video with your lover... excited? Videos aren't only for Paris and Kim anymore! Set up a tripod near your bed (I don't love the idea of filming on your phone, Heaven forbid that gets sent out accidentally or your phone gets hacked!) Break the ice by putting on some cheesy porno music and film yourselves goin' to town.

There are many different kinds of sex videos you can make. Maybe you want to make a really wild video. When I think of wild, one word that comes to mind is fisting. However, as most of you know, there may not be enough tape in your video camera because if you are a fan of fisting you know it takes a long time before it can be accomplished. For those of you who may need a refresher course, it's best to start by making out a lot so that you are both very turned on and lubed up. Start slowly-one finger, then two and graduate your way up to getting your whole hand up inside your girl's vagina. Just be focused on her and what she wants. Remind her to breathe and take it slow, slow, slow! Getting a close of view of this with the camera is definitely wild.

Fetish videos are quite popular in the sex industry. Maybe on part of the video you will be up for trying a little spanking. Some of my friends are really into this. One of my friends swears that being spanked in just the right area (her lower bottom) instantly sends a sexual sensation that she feels deep inside her vagina. Some women like it to sting just a little, some like to be spanked with an object such as a ruler, the list goes on and on. Try it out if your partner is game.

While the tape is rolling, why not keep a few secrets up your sleeve and see her surprised reaction for the first time on film. Why not have a pair of handcuffs under the pillow to whip out? Tell your girl to trust you, slip them on her (make sure if you purchase the kind with a key you don't lose it or this really will be an eventful night!) and have your way with her. Switch it up, at times bite and nibble her nipples, slide a well lubed finger up her ass, tickle her…whatever you think may be unexpected and welcomed. Really get out of your comfort zone and have FUN. If at any time she tells you to stop, immediately uncuff her and wait for her cue on what she wants to do next. She may surprise you!

For you pseudo-actors out there, why not pretend you are in one of those awful porno movies where a woman is sitting alone at home having a lonely evening with her television when oh no, the television breaks! What's a lonely girl to do? She calls the TV repairman and low and behold he wants to do her! What a surprise! Well, why not dress up in a cap, a pair of overalls and one of those hysterical 70's mustaches and try to fix your girlfriend's...um, television. Simply set up the camera as a long shot and act it all out. It will be a lot of fun to watch later and while it may just make you laugh- chances are it will get you aroused to see how your bodies look from the outside looking in. Or you may cringe seeing yourself on screen that way—that's okay too. It's all about connecting and connect you will!

Chapter Twenty-Nine

Day 26- Cool Girlfriends Plan Yearly Honeymoons

What do couples do on their honeymoon? All together now…they have sex! Right! Having something to look forward to where sex is actually scheduled allows you both time to really plan for great sex. Time alone to rediscover why you fell in love in the first place is critical to sustaining a working relationship. Sex trips sound kind of contrived, so we shall call it a honeymoon. I want you to sit down with your honey and a calendar and plan a honeymoon every year going forward.

I want you to celebrate your love with a trip that is about just the two of you. Make lists of the things you will do, the places you will see and the sex moves you are going to try out on each other. Our lives get very hectic so setting aside actual scheduled time for sex is often necessary. It doesn't sound very romantic though does it? That's where the honeymoon part comes in. A getaway to a country inn or an African safari will always be romantic because it's a time for you and your woman to dedicate entirely to each other. Don't feel it has to be overly adventurous, but it has to be a change from your routine. A spa weekend can be great or even an intensive tennis camp getaway can be a hoot.

Why not simply take a road trip and disappear? Be adventurous! Take a road trip and hit every flea market along the way. If you have the means, go to Asia or some other distant country. Take a long train ride to a place on the map you have never been before.

If you simply don't have the funds for an all out honeymoon why not plan a road trip somewhere local? Or a staycation where you turn off from the world and turn on your girl? Think of all the fun you can have in the car singing songs and playing games. You can stop off at local dive bars and just soak up the flavor of small towns. Make sure to bring tunes you love. My favorite road trip song is hearing Melissa Etheridge sing "You Can Sleep While I Drive." Pop that baby in on the road and if it does the same for you girls as it does for me, you will be well on your way to having the right roadie mindset. Have fun ladies and don't forget to send a post card from the road!

Chapter Thirty

Day 27- Cool Girlfriends Eat Out

    We are into the home stretch now, chapter Dirty Thirty! Tonight you will be eating out which happens as you eat in. Call your girl and tell her you have a special dinner planned for tonight. When she gets home serve her a favorite meal. Greet her with a cold drink. Keep eye contact and enjoy light conversation. Flirt a little. Reach out and touch her during dinner, feed her a taste of the food you have ordered in or prepared. Keep it sensual. Then tell her dessert is waiting in the bedroom. But in order to receive it she must agree to allow herself to completely surrender to you. Tonight is all about her. Tell her that your pleasure will come from seeing her pleasured. Instruct her to lie down on the bed on her stomach. Put some sexy music on and give her a full body massage. After she has become completely relaxed flip her over and start kissing her everywhere except in her genital area. Give attention to every inch of her body, moving slowly and softly. Then when you are satisfied not one area of her body has been missed, begin by licking around her inner lips and perineum. Always keep your hands moving, let one hand caress her breasts, moving to her lips, let her suck on one of your fingers. If she starts to go on autopilot to give back some attention to you remind her that all you need from her is to lay back and enjoy the ride. I don't need to tell you how to go down on your woman, as I know my readers aren't novices. So let me give you a few ideas to try that perhaps you haven't done in awhile.

While you are caressing her body, begin licking around her clit. We all know how sensitive it can be and rushing is never a good idea. Be acutely aware of how her body is answering your movements. If her pelvis starts to lift, if she is moaning or rocking, you can assume you are on the right path.

When you were having regular sex with your girl, you probably found out what she likes and what turns her off. Stored in your memory bank there should be a treasure trove of erogenous zones that you have found to pleasure her. Use your tongue the way she loves it in the places she loves to feel it. Then pump it up a notch.

Have a hot (not too hot) washcloth in a bowl of warm water nearby. Stop licking her for a moment allowing your mouth to pause for a few seconds away from her body, and submerge the washcloth in the warm water...at this point it shouldn't be hot—just warm. Drape it over her vagina. Make sure she is sufficiently warmed up. Squeeze out the remaining hot water over her pussy, let it drizzle over her. Then put a few ice cubes into your mouth. Go back to licking her. Try tracing out the alphabet around her clit. The warm feeling she will be experiencing coupled with the coldness of your mouth should send her into orbit. She just may want this sensation every night. Send her soaring out of the depths of LBD and back into your arms again.

Chapter Thirty-One

Day 28- Cool Girlfriends Go Shopping- Strap Ons, Butt Plugs and Edible Panties OH MY!

A visit to the sex shop can be a tremendously yummy treat! That's where I am sending you both today! Get a big basket and load up the following…

Vibrators- A girl's best friend? Quite possibly! The most impressive thing that vibrators have going for them is they will usually get the job done—that can't always be said for our lovers. They provide just the right amount of pressure, strength and rhythm to ensure a happy ending almost every time without fail. Vibrators can be taken into your bed at anytime but they come in especially handy when you get home from a long day at work and just don't feel up to going down on your woman but want to see her satisfied.

Vibrators come in many varieties; some you can plug in, some run on batteries, some can go up inside you. I suggest experimenting with them all. You will probably find that each one delivers a completely different orgasm. You can use them alone or incorporate them into lovemaking. Vibrators are the old standby and get many women through some difficult lonely times. Nobody ever really has anything bad to say about them and no matter what anyone says, almost everyone owns one. It may also float your boat to purchase a "remote control pulsating vibrating toy." Go online or to your local sex shop and you will find a number of companies that are making hands-free, multi-function, quiet, pulsating and vibrating remote control panties! Those geniuses at sex shops really know their stuff, don't they! I want you to wrap this gift and have her slide on her new undies and take her out to dinner. Have fun pushing the button, which will activate the vibration – so long as you stay within a twenty-foot range. It runs on batteries and while they don't provide all that much of a punch, it certainly adds a new dimension to dinner out! Enjoy!

Dildos- Dildos are almost always a popular bedfellow with lesbians. Why not go and buy one in a crazy color or a different size from what you may be used to using (if you have used one that is). Since we are kind of starting anew here, a new dildo would be a smart purchase. I probably don't have to remind you when choosing one, that silicone is often the dildo of choice because you can throw them in the dishwasher. If it has been awhile since you have incorporated a dildo into your sex play, why not try it tonight? You don't need to start by strapping it on— perhaps that is too much work for tonight. Just holding it in your hand and playing with different levels and kinds of penetration can be a lot of fun. Working a strap on takes core strength and a bit of practice, but every woman can learn just by having patience and will. Ask your girlfriend if she wants you to slide it in slowly or if she wants you to "fuck her brains out"—that should give you more than a clue as to the kind of rhythm you should be using. Maybe learn to make it an extension of your body and really learn how to work that thing. Try slipping a condom over it. You can use your hands or show off a little. Practice putting the condom in your mouth and putting it on without using your hands. This always looks sexy.

Dual Dildos- Double the pleasure, double the fun! For you adventurous types, why not get a two-headed dildo and share it! This provides you both with the opportunity to each get penetrated while playing with each other's breasts or fingering each other's genitals. You can either both have the dildo in your vaginas or try sliding it in the backdoor. Just make sure you stick to one hole. Bacteria should never get near your vagina.

There are many positions you can try with this double duty dildo so have fun and experiment!

Butt Plugs- Butt plugs need lube like a fish needs water. Make sure that if you are putting something into your ass (or your lady's), you do it carefully. And never put anything that has been used for ass play anywhere else. Some women just like the feeling of having a butt plug up inside them—they get high from the way it stimulates the nerve endings in and around their anus. Butt plugs come in many different sizes and girths, so experiment until you find one that speaks to you both. Some like it in for a short while, others like wearing them for hours. Some women enjoy having a butt plug pulled out at the moment they orgasm. Find out if your girlfriend likes how it feels to tug on it as you play with her, or twist it around. If you haven't been paying proper attention to your lady's fine ass, start now. Just make sure the base is large enough that you can actually get it out… Not a fun trip to the emergency room should it get stuck!

Anal Beads- Beads aren't just for necklaces anymore! Anal beads are simply a few beads strung together on a piece of string. I have seen beads that are all the same size and color and some that increase in size.

Try placing each bead one at a time up inside your girlfriend's butt or she can do it herself. The beads stimulate all those nerve endings in your behind. You can use them when you are performing oral sex on her and then the moment she starts to come pull those babies out. Then try them yourself. It may not be Mardi Gras but it's going to be a wild night full of beads!

Nipple Clamps- By now you should be very familiar with how sensitive your woman's breasts are. Some women levitate outside their bodies when theirs are touched and played with; some feel almost nothing at all. Even the most gentle nipple clamps can't be called comfortable but if you haven't tried them out, it may be something fun to discover together. Many varieties of clamps can be tightened or loosened depending on your level of tolerance.

Pinwheels- If you are really feeling bad to the bone, you can buy a pinwheel, which is a bit of a punishment tool that some women, especially S/M ladies, seem to squeal over. The pinwheel is a stainless steel wheel that won't puncture the skin (if held at a careful slant) that can be used to send varying degrees of pleasure or pain when wheeled around the body and genitals.

Handcuffs- As mentioned in the video section, bondage is also something you can "tie up" your time with tonight. This can be especially "bonding" because it requires a huge amount of trust. Once we hand over our control to someone else we are telling her that we trust her without hesitation. Some women enjoy feeling submissive and will beg for some punishment. If she is game, try some gentle biting and twisting of her nipples. Some women enjoy light slapping on their breasts. If you enjoy this, just make sure you have some keywords that mean stop. Be sure the rules will be obeyed and that if it gets too intense the game can be stopped whenever one person says the keyword.

Dripping candles- Hot wax can be incorporated into your night of passion if a bit of pain floats your boat. The hot wax can be dripped over her (or your) body but do this with caution and please keep it away from your lovely faces, ladies.

Edible Underthings- Why not revisit the swingin' 70s and purchase some of those edible panties or boxers that were so popular back then? Hey, I love food—especially candy—so I'm not going to knock it. And until you try it, neither should you!

Simone Reyes

Lucky for us there will always be new toys to play with so keep looking online and at your local sex shop until there is something that catches your eye. A field trip to the sex shop should be high on your list of priorities. Make it a point to plan a visit at least every few months. Keep shakin' it up in the bedroom and it will become your LBD kryptonite.

Like a kid with a pumpkin full of candy on Halloween turn off all distractions, open up your treats and dive right in, baby… the water is fine!!

Chapter Thirty-Two

Day 29 –Cool Girlfriends Dig Quickies

Sometimes short, quick sex is just what the doctor ordered. Today I want you to get to know the neighborhood in a way you never have before. See how much action you can get going in secret—but in public. For example, go to the grocery store, in the frozen foods section, when nobody is looking why not let your girlfriend sneak a peek at your breast? Your nipples will look especially erect with the chill there. So flash her!

When you are at the bookstore, try hiding behind a wall of books and copping a feel. When you are out to lunch disappear into the bathroom together, into the same stall and grind each other to climax.

Jump in your car and see if you can park somewhere private and engage in a quickie when nobody is looking. Or if you don't have a car, take a cab and mutually pleasure each other when the driver isn't looking (just make sure you are ducked down far enough so s/he can't see you in the rear view mirror).

Go shopping for a new outfit and sneak into the dressing room together. As you are trying on new outfits slip your fingers down her pants and have your own private party in the room.

Go to her office or place of business allow your lover to believe you are taking her out to lunch but instead drive her home, have lunch laid out on the bed and take turns feeding each other— getting in a quickie before the hour is up.

You get the game; quickies are very exciting and get you both used to seeing every moment of every day as potential time for lovemaking.

Chapter Thirty-Three

Day 30- Cool Girlfriends Play Twister Every night

All you have to say is "Honey, let's play Twister." You won't need the board game as in the previous chapter; just grab a few of these position suggestions and have at it! I am envious of you both tonight! What fun you are both going to have! Trying out new sex positions is a stellar way to broaden your sexual repertoire. It doesn't matter how long you have been in a relationship, trying new positions opens up a whole new level of pleasure possibilities. Some positions involve submission and domination, some taste; some allow us to look deeply into our lover's eyes making a spiritual connection while others are just pure animal. I feel it's always best to start out with a lot of slow kissing before ever reaching for the breasts or genital area. However, some women really do like it rough, so it's really up to the individual. Our bodies are filled with hidden erogenous zones and it's up to our partners to find them.

Remember, if any of these positions seem awkward or you fall out of them and end up on the floor, just laugh it off—sex is meant to be fun after all! It is how adults play, so don't take it too seriously!

Begin tonight by dimming the lights, playing her favorite music, lighting candles and relaxing together. Kiss your lover slowly and passionately and then tell her you want to try something new. Maybe you will try one of these tonight or maybe you will try them all. Whatever you decide just take it slow, savor every moment and have a good time.

Position # 1- The Thelma and Louise- Louise is laying face up. Half of her body is on the floor (resting her shoulders and upper body on the floor) with her head resting on a comfy pillow and half on your bed. Louise's legs are bent, with her hips, legs and ass up on the bedspread apart for Thelma's enjoyment. It kind of looks like a half headstand- but using the bed for support. Thelma is on the bed, stomach down, facing Louise with precious access to her lover's sacred place. Thelma can lie down across the bed and use her tongue to pleasure Louise. Louise can move her pelvis around to meet Thelma's tongue thrusts in and out of her vagina. In this position, it's all about Louise and her pleasure. Lucky Louise!

Position #2- The Legs and Goldie –This position is so special because it incorporates the spooning position that everyone gets so much comfort from with their special someone. Both Legs and Goldie are lying on their side with Legs facing front and her woman, Goldie, facing the back of Legs' head. Goldie reaches her arm around to reach Leg's clit, while Legs raises her leg to make her private area more accessible. Goldie and Legs are able to kiss passionately—all it requires is for Legs to look over her shoulder. In this position, Goldie can use one hand to pass over Leg's shoulder to play with her breast while her other hand is free to rub Leg's clit until she comes.

Position # 3- The Violet and Corky- This position rocks because Corky gets to do Violet in a hardcore, animal way, which is always a great break from the norm. Violet is on all fours and Corky is wearing a dildo. Corky is behind Violet, holding onto Violet's hair. Corky gently inserts the dildo into Violet's pussy, penetrating her from behind, directing the dildo in the direction of Violet's G- Spot. Violet can add to her good time by touching herself.

Position # 4- The Vivian and Cay- This wonderful position is so popular because it gives Vivian a chance to show off her fine booty to her girl. Vivian lies on her back with her legs up and spread apart. Cay is on top of Vivian, straddling Vivian's hips in a reverse pose- with her ass in Vivian's reach. Cay and Vivian are hip to hip. Cay's head falls between Vivian's legs so that she can pleasure her, while Vivian has full access to Cay's behind. Cay's ass is tilted upward allowing Vivian to play with Cay's behind, lick her there; whatever she feels will pleasure Cay. She can also insert a finger or a toy into Cay's anus. Vivian can give Cay a little spank and tickle if the mood strikes. Cay can suck on Vivian's clitoris or insert a finger or two into her vagina if she so desires.

Position # 5- The Kelly and Brenda- This position requires a bit of agility on the part of Kelly, but it's worth the extra work because Brenda gets the best view ever of her lover's sacred spot. Kelly is lying on her back, her head resting on a pillow. Brenda is facing her, kneeling in front of her. Kelly's legs are wrapped around Brenda's neck giving a perfect view of Kelly's vagina. Brenda gently inserts one finger at a time into Kelly's pussy, eventually working up to two fingers, then three and so on. Kelly is free to pleasure herself as she watches Brenda's fingers disappear inside her pussy. Brenda can easily bring Kelly to climax while having the best view of her beautiful girlfriend.

Position # 6- The Lucy And Ethel- This position only requires a bed and a desire to please. Both ladies get to come at the same time if they want to try to plan that. Sometimes that works, sometimes it doesn't but it's always fun to try! Ethel is lying on her back with her legs wrapped around the hips of Lucy who is sitting, facing her. Ethel's breasts are completely accessible to Lucy, as is her pussy. One of Lucy's hands can play with her lover's breasts, putting her nipple between her fingers and tugging on them. Her other hand is pleasuring Ethel's pussy by rubbing her clit and inserting a few fingers into her vagina until she climaxes.

Position # 7 - The Blair and Jo- This position is a blast because Jo gets to control how much of Blair she wants inside of her—it's Jo's world and Blair gets a great view of her lady in action. Blair is lying on her back and her girl Jo is on top of her facing away from Blair. Blair is holding onto Jo's round hips. Blair is wearing a strap-on. Jo is on top of Blair facing away with her legs straddled around her lover's hips in a sitting position. Blair's hands are on Jo's hips guiding her up and down on her "cock." Using her lover's guidance, Jo lowers herself over Blair's hard on. Jo can ride her lover allowing for little or deep penetration. Jo has both of her hands free to caress her own breasts and clit as Blair's dildo fills her, providing much enjoyment.

Position # 8- The Adele and Emma- I think this position is so great because it can (and should!) be used after a lusty lap dance... Hey, you are already in the chair, right? Emma is seated in a chair with Adele on her lap facing her. Adele's legs are spread apart, with her knees squeezing Emma's torso. Emma is facing Adele's lovely breasts, so she can flick her tongue around Emma's nipples, suck on them and play with them. In turn, Adele can use this position to rub her body against Adele's, getting clitoral stimulation from Emma's hands, which are free to rub and enter her lover. This position allows both women to really get close. They can gaze into each other's eyes and kiss deeply while they get it on.

Position # 9- The Laverne and Shirley - Remember gymnastics when you were a kid? Well, it's time to get into that head space because this move is a muscle move. Once you master it, you will return to it often! Laverne needs some strong legs for this, but I have faith in you girls. This position looks a bit like straddling a horse except your woman is face up. Laverne is laying on her back on the edge of the bed. Laverne's butt and legs are off the bed hovering over the floor. She may need to be on her tiptoes depending on how high the bed is. Laverne's back is straight, resembling a table. Shirley is sitting on top of her with her legs falling down over each of Laverne's hips reaching the floor. For balance, the women can hold hands. Or Shirley can play with Laverne's breasts. Both women can grind each other in this position, which may bring each Laverne and Shirley to climax. If not, Shirley can easily slide her body farther down, with her head at Laverne's pussy and go to town!

Position # 10- The Wonder Woman and Etta Candy: This position makes the girl in the Wonder Woman role feel on top of the world- because she is! Joe Cocker sings, "Stand on that chair, yeah, that's right," so why not use that song tonight for direction. Etta stands up on a chair—be sure to position the chair near a wall because when she gets her groove on, she may tumble right off of it! Wonder Woman is standing in front of her lover, face at pussy level. Etta's leg is draped over Wonder Woman's shoulder. Wonder Woman's hand is free to reach up to cup and caress Etta's breasts. She can also twist and play with Etta's nipples as Etta steadies herself by putting her hands on Wonder Woman's head, with her fingers in her hair. Wonder Woman licks and sucks on Etta's pussy until she makes that woman fly.

Chapter Thirty-Four

Day 31- Cool Girlfriends Have Great Sex

Graduation Day!!!!!!!! Oh, I am so proud of you...of both of you! Give yourself a big pat on the back—no, on the ass! You gals deserve it! Now that you have flipped the switch back to the on position you can really begin to enjoy your partnership. No longer will you have to feel sexually unfulfilled and endure that pain in silence. Now you will reach for your vibrator because you want to, not because you need to. Best of all, you will have a deeper, more profound connection with your lover.

Enjoy this time. Indulge each other; talk about how it feels to be reconnecting, touch each other often in sexual ways. Remember to laugh together when you are in bed, reminisce about last night's great sex, and just enjoy it. It won't always be easy- this is like a honeymoon period—there will always be more work to do but now you have the tools to do it. I am sure that by now all of your hard work and dedication is being showered right back at you. When there is true love in a relationship, it often just takes one partner to give a bit more of herself to elicit the same reaction from the other.

My wish for you is that you continue to celebrate your union daily. Continue to leave those sweet notes and give foot rubs freely. Make love when you feel love. Give your lover pleasure slowly and with feeling. Or if you are both in the mood, don't make love—just fuck. Making love and fucking are not identical. When we make love, it's a spiritual connection but sometimes we just want to feel flesh against flesh and that is okay. There is nothing wrong with a quick fuck. There will always be appointments to keep, businesses to run, family obligations to tend to, but out of all the things we should skimp on, sex is not one of them. If going to sleep without connecting sexually has become a habit, well, habits are meant to be broken.

Sex is a vital part of any relationship. It is often a barometer of how well the relationship is going and if it is destined to last. There are always going to be ebbs and flows but let's keep the flowing going. What we give is what we get. You have the tools to restart this engine. You have followed my advice in these chapters and taken a stand to help heal your partnership. In many

Slaying the Lesbian Bed Death Dragon

ways you have already won the battle just by being present in the desire to create real change in your relationship. Be still in your life. Stop to smell the roses. Never let ego rule you. Never let fear rule you. Be brave. Live the life you love. Love the life you live. Never settle. Be yourself. Stand proud. Respect her. Respect yourself. Be open. Never judge. Practice compassion. Have faith. Be kind. And continue to love your woman the best way you know how.

Part 3: I've Got My Lover Back…Now What?

Cool Girlfriends Keep The Fire Burning

Now that you have reclaimed your lover and sent that Lesbian Bed Death Dragon packing, you may be faced with the fear induced question, "Now what?" Well, now comes the even harder part. You must keep that torch lit. This means simply keeping this book near your bed and referring to it often. It also means keeping your journal handy and continuing to use it daily.

Never again forget that you are blessed to have this woman in your life. Never feel so secure in your relationship that you don't fear her leaving you for someone else. Never get so comfortable that you don't want to look your best for her. Never take her for granted. Never give in to feeling too tired to spoil her, indulge her fantasies and awaken her sexual goddess. Never stop trying to impress her, wow her, and make her smile. Never allow your insecurity or anger to get away from you. Always unload it first onto your journal. Never keep your feelings bottled up—just present them to your lover in a calm, sane way. Never allow your loneliness or insecurity to get so big that you find yourself seeking the love what you want from your lover with another woman. Never walk with your head down through your house. It is your castle and you must take your woman by the hand and dance through it. Never forget that you must always be a student; your woman will always be changing, so keep up with your studies.

Do discover new ways to please her. Do find new curves in her body, new moves that send her flying, new words that speak to her heart. Do your best to connect with her daily. Lock eyes with her, leave notes in her wallet, speak and read to her erotically. Do remember to touch her, kiss her and make love to her. Do make every moment with her special and always view her as more than a special friend. She is your girlfriend, your wife, your lover, your everything—let her know this. Make her believe how you feel about her because she can feel it in your kiss. Take care of her and she will take care of you, in and outside of the bedroom. Love your woman with all your heart, body and soul and reap the rewards. Forever.

What if Issues Still Remain?

Simone Reyes

This is the hardest chapter to write. However, it would be irresponsible and narcissistic for me to think I have all the answers for every lesbian couple on the planet. All relationships are different and some do have an expiration date. Sometimes, even if we have sex with our partner again or engage in it more frequently, something still feels like it is missing. Something still feels forced or unnatural. Sometimes we still know that we need and yearn for something more. Sometimes our relationship simply cannot provide for our needs anymore. Sometimes we stay out of obligation. Sometimes we stay out of fear. Sometimes we stay because we are afraid of being alone. Sometimes we stay because we are afraid we can't do better. Too often we stay because it is comfortable.

These are not reasons to stay. They are about co-dependence. Co-dependent relationships dress up as love but they are not love. Don't fall for the disguise. There are moments when the void is just too big and our needs are just not being satisfied. Sometimes love just isn't enough. And that is ok.

There are times when all the books, intention candles, therapy and wishing won't put Humpty Dumpy back together again. And it sucks. We have all been here:

the awful, tear your heart out moment when we know in our soul that it's really over. Sadly, it is not usually the case that both women come to this conclusion at the same time. One is usually labeled the "victim" and one the "monster"—neither label is usually fair or accurate, as we all know. I have been both and I know how I have felt in each circumstance. I can say that neither are enviable positions to be in.

Personally, on the few occasions I have really had my heart shredded, I have been known to stay in bed for days on end, either eat like a maniac or stop eating entirely. I want to sleep all the time or I suffer from terrible insomnia. I have recurring nightmares that haunt my sleep with images of the girl that got away. And of course there are many tears, often when you least expect them. I recall reading an article where a psychologist described just dumped patients in his office as looking like patients recovering from an operation or car accident. There are inevitable feelings of rejection, shame, disbelief, anger, rage etc., not to mention, my own personal favorite—denial. As cliché as it sounds, the only remedy is time and acceptance. Gather your friends around you and try to take care of the small things; the bigger things will have to wait. Seek professional help if you need it.

I know many women think that jumping into another relationship is the best cure for a broken heart. It certainly does ease the pain to have some pretty shiny new girl to distract you, but you must ask yourself if it is really fair to yourself (not to mention the rebound girl) in the long run. Often, rebound relationships are a temporary band-aid for pain that we must all endure and work through. People often put all their hopes onto this new conquest, deciding that she can save them, then the woman becomes real and they are again left to deal with many of the same issues as they had in their past relationship. They break up with that person and the cycle continues. Or worse, the side chick who is constantly playing nursemaid during difficult times becomes the wife, all in an attempt to never deal with the demons that live inside of all of us. Protect yourself from these relationships and do the work on yourself first. Make peace with being alone. Fall in love with your own company. You will be better equipped to deal with someone new once you have thoroughly worked through your own heartbreak.

On the upside, (and yes, there is an upside!) lesbians merge so fully and share such deep, complicated relationships with their partner that we often do remain friends where other couples do not. We have all heard about our lesbian friends taking vacations and spending the holidays together after the pain of their break up has subsided. Fortunately, even when it is decided that the love affair must end it is not entirely uncommon for us to remain part of our extended family (unless of course trust and respect have been compromised too severely by abuse or infidelity).

I have found the hardest relationships to get over are the ones where the person you cared for simply cuts you from their life and makes you invisible. Suddenly someone who professed to be your trusted friend/confidant/lover becomes an instant stranger. Conflict-avoiders often use this as their way out. It seems like the cruelest way to walk out of someone's life, even when it is done for self-protection. If possible, try to remember that we are all flawed; we all have moments we would like to take back and at least for a time we were the person you cared for the most. If we can all remember this, perhaps the pain of the relationship ending will have a hopeful future for the two of you to remain in each other's lives as friends. Sometimes things fall apart so that they can come back together again at a later date and time. Sometimes you have to take a chance on getting back with an ex to really realize why it didn't work out every other time and free yourself to love someone new who may be waiting for you somewhere out there. We never know. Just don't waste your time or another person's by trying to make something work that is fatally flawed. Be with the girl who sets your heart AND your pants on fire. And be okay to be alone. As I often read on Instagram feeds, "Never settle for less than butterflies." I certainly never have.

Maybe your wife or girlfriend isn't The One. Maybe the girl of your dreams is someone you have yet to meet. Maybe she is someone from your past who still holds a piece of your heart. Or maybe one day you and your girlfriend will find each other looking into each other's eyes again. We never know what fate has in store for us, but we must believe everything happens for a reason and will leave us stronger women in the end. Let go of what isn't meant for you.

For now, the lesson is to get to know yourself. Perhaps, for the first time the gift is recognizing that you can be a complete and happy woman alone. There are many single-by-choice women in the world or those who are on (wo)mancations where they become their own best friend and partner. Loving ourselves and enjoying our own company is vital to living a healthy life when in a partnership or in between lovers. Many of us have still grown up with the idea that unless we are partnered up, we are somehow lacking in our lives. This is a myth and a dangerous one at that. If you do not learn how to feel comfortable and at peace being alone it is entirely possible your panic will result in making choices that are unhealthy. It is no surprise that a person's yearning for companionship at any cost causes them to settle. Perhaps they push all their partner's flaws under the rug because at least they are there. Or they may know in their gut that their spouse has manipulated them or lied to them but they forgive it because then they won't be alone. Clearly this is a toxic way to go through life. Having faith in yourself and waiting for the right person to come along beats trying to mold the wrong person into that role just because you are afraid of the unknown. If this sounds familiar, I urge you to bet on yourself. You may have some uncomfortable nights, you may feel lonely and that is okay. It is during these difficult times when we truly learn how strong we are. It is when we are tested that we do the work on ourselves that guarantees that we will never choose someone out of any emotion except true love. Work on yourself may include therapy, energy work, hypnosis, connecting with a spiritual community, reading self help books, meditating, the list goes on and on. The journey may be hard, but it is worth it. And from this work you will be in the right frame of mind to make choices you can be proud of and that will nurture your soul. I wish that for you.

Always take care of you. Be kind to yourself and continue to believe in love.

About the Author

Simone Reyes was the breakout star of Oxygen's reality TV show "Running Russell Simmons" and became an overnight hero in the animal rights community. She has been entertainment mogul, Russell Simmons, right hand woman since high school and has often been affectionately referred to as the "Boss" by Simmons himself.

She was recently promoted to Director of Television Development at Simmons' Def Pictures media company. Simone boldly shed her clothes for PETA's "Rather Go Naked" demonstrations and Stray Cat Alliance and has used her voice in countless media outlets to speak out in support of animal liberation.

She is a well known speaker on animal rights at events such as The Seed in NYC, WorldFest, National Animal Rights Conference alongside the founding leaders in the animal rights movement. Simone's Tedx talk has inspired many viewers to try veganism and re-think their treatment of animals. Simone is a 20+ year vegan and has been a grassroots animal rights activist for most of her adult life. PETA's Animal Rahat Sanctuary in India was officially given a new name "Simone's Place" in honor of Simone's tireless dedication to the animal rights cause.

Simone Reyes

Last year she traveled to Taiji, Japan as a Sea Shepherd Cove Guardian to report on and document the atrocities of the dolphin drives. She shared her experiences there in various media outlets including HLN/Jane Velez Mitchell's show. She, along with Russell Simmons penned an open letter to Ambassador Caroline Kennedy and President Obama urging them to consider attaching the plight of the dolphins who migrate through Japan to the passing of the Trans Pacific Partnership- this letter was signed by dozens of celebrities including Cher, Oliver Stone, Charlize Theron, Sean Penn, Susan Sarandon, Cameron Diaz, Reverend Jesse Jackson and countless others.

She has also been honored by Mercy For Animals for the work she has done to put the plight of farm animals in the public's consciousness. She has been has been featured in print and online at Star Magazine, OK magazine, Inked Magazine, Our Hen House, peta.com , Supreme Master TV, Veg News Magazine, Vegetarian Times, True Cowboy Magazine and countless other publications/blogs and has appeared on television shows/movies including Extra, Entertainment Tonight, Dogs In The City, MTV News, Sky vs. Sky, The Ellen DeGeneres Show, The L Word, The L Word Special, The Wendy Williams Show, and most recently Simone played herself on HBO's "Enlightened".

Simone also serves on the board of Social Compassion In Legislation. She is a regular contributor to websites Global Grind, Hello Giggles and One Green Planet. Simone uses her voice to inspire, motivate, mobilize and guide people who care about the treatment of animals but don't know where to begin to create real change for them.

She is the author of "Astrology For Dogs" and "Astrology For Cats". She lives in Los Angeles with her senior, rescued, blind Japanese Chin, Hubbell Yoda, who is her best friend.

Twitter: @simonereyes
Facebook: facebook.com/activistsimonereyes
Instagram: @simonereyes
Periscope: @simonereyes
Website: simonereyes.com

www.tri-pub.com

www.ingramcontent.com/pod-product-compliance
Lightning Source LLC
LaVergne TN
LVHW051553070426
835507LV00021B/2551